Jodie Davis

Paper-Pieced

Bed Quilts

Martingale™
& COMPANY

Credits

PRESIDENT · *Nancy J. Martin*
CEO · *Daniel J. Martin*
PUBLISHER · *Jane Hamada*
EDITORIAL DIRECTOR · *Mary V. Green*
MANAGING EDITOR · *Tina Cook*
TECHNICAL EDITOR · *Karen Soltys*
COPY EDITOR · *Allison A. Merrill*
DESIGN AND PRODUCTION MANAGER · *Stan Green*
ILLUSTRATOR · *Robin Strobel*
COVER DESIGNER · *Stan Green*
TEXT DESIGNER · *Trina Stahl*
PHOTOGRAPHER · *Brent Kane*

That Patchwork Place® is an imprint of
Martingale & Company™.

Paper-Pieced Bed Quilts
© 2001 by Jodie Davis

Martingale & Company
20205 144th Avenue NE
Woodinville, WA 98072-8478 USA
www.martingale-pub.com

Printed in China
06 05 04 03 02 01   8 7 6 5 4 3 2 1

Mission Statement

We are dedicated to providing quality products and service by working together to inspire creativity and to enrich the lives we touch.

Library of Congress Cataloging-in-Publication Data

Davis, Jodie.
    Paper-pieced bed quilts / Jodie Davis.
        p.   cm.
    ISBN 1–56477–395–7
    1. Patchwork—Patterns.   2. Quilting—Patterns.   I. Title.

TT835 .D3746978 2001
746.46'041—dc21
                                                        2001044168

Dedication

To Neukitty

In appreciation for all those long hours that you spent in my lap blessing each of these quilts with a proper breaking-in as I hand stitched the bindings.

Acknowledgments

This book was certainly a group effort. I couldn't have dreamed of completing it in the few short months it took without the help of many people.

Thanks to Joann Spiers, Janet Peterson, Michele Bautsch, and Tammy Silvers, who pieced quilt tops, and to machine quilters Glenda Irvine, Sylvia Davis, Sue Hunston, and Karen Williams, who quilted the projects on their long-arm machines. Tammy Silvers also created the lovely hand-dyed fabrics used in "Potted Posies" on page 54.

My appreciation goes to the members of the online guild FoundationPiecers for indulging me in market research. Thanks also to the members of the Bulloch Hall quilt guild who tested my patterns during a delightful day spent to the tune of humming sewing machines.

Contents

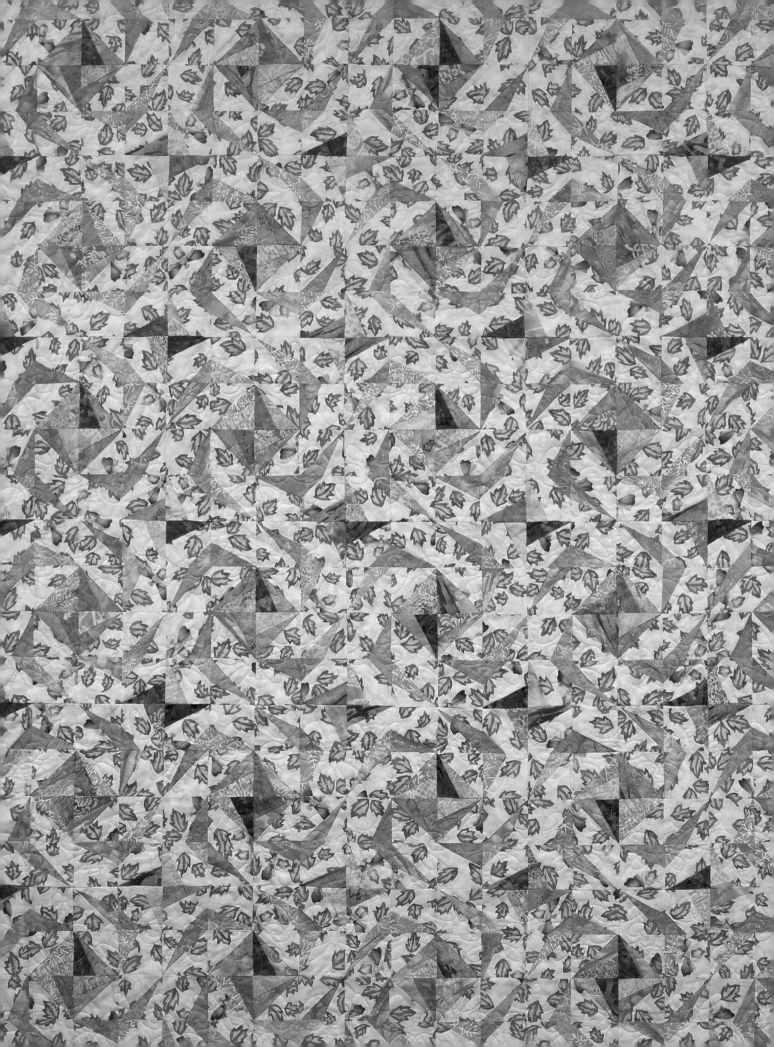

Preface

Why paper piece bed quilts?

After writing a half-dozen books about paper piecing wall-size projects over the last few years, I was hankering for some quilts for my bed. Having finished my last book, I rewarded myself by reproducing a quilt top following a design I'd seen on eBay (an Internet auction site). About halfway through the piecing, having already corrected a number of mismatched points, it struck me that I'd rather paper piece even this simple design, to make it easier to match all the points and to avoid problems with bias edges stretching.

Wondering whether I was just an overly fanatic paper-piecer, I queried members of FoundationPiecers, an on-line quilting group. Sure enough, the e-mail replies revealed that I was not alone. Many paper-piecers told me they also made bed-size quilts using this technique, often enlarging small paper-piecing patterns to do so. I didn't need more of an invitation than that to start this book!

Introduction

You will find everything you need to know to create your quilt in the pages of this book, so that even if you've never paper pieced before, you'll be able to succeed. First I cover the basics of paper piecing, then progress to the ins and outs of constructing your quilt top. Finishing instructions complete the how-to section.

Equipped with these basics, you're ready to begin making any of the eight quilts. You'll find full-size block patterns as well as quilt layouts for twin, queen (which generally will fit a full-size bed too), and king sizes of each design, plus yardage and cutting charts, along with a color photo of each quilt. Complete, detailed instructions with illustrations guide you through the creation of the quilts.

A long-arm quilting machine was used to quilt each of the quilts in this book. As I hear more and more often, many quilters love to piece or appliqué, but either don't have the time or don't wish to hand or machine quilt. I myself enjoy machine quilting smaller projects, but when it comes to a bed-size quilt, I turn it over to the experts. In the instructions for each quilt, I have given the name of the quilt pattern used by the quilter. These designs are well known among long-arm machine quilters, so your local quilter should be able to reproduce the same designs on your quilt if you so desire. Of course, if you love to hand or machine quilt, by all means enjoy the process!

Finally, you won't want to miss "Resources," starting on page 77. You'll find tried-and-true mail-order and Internet fabric and quilting supply sources, plus some of my favorite quilting Web sites, chock-full of information. Let's get started!

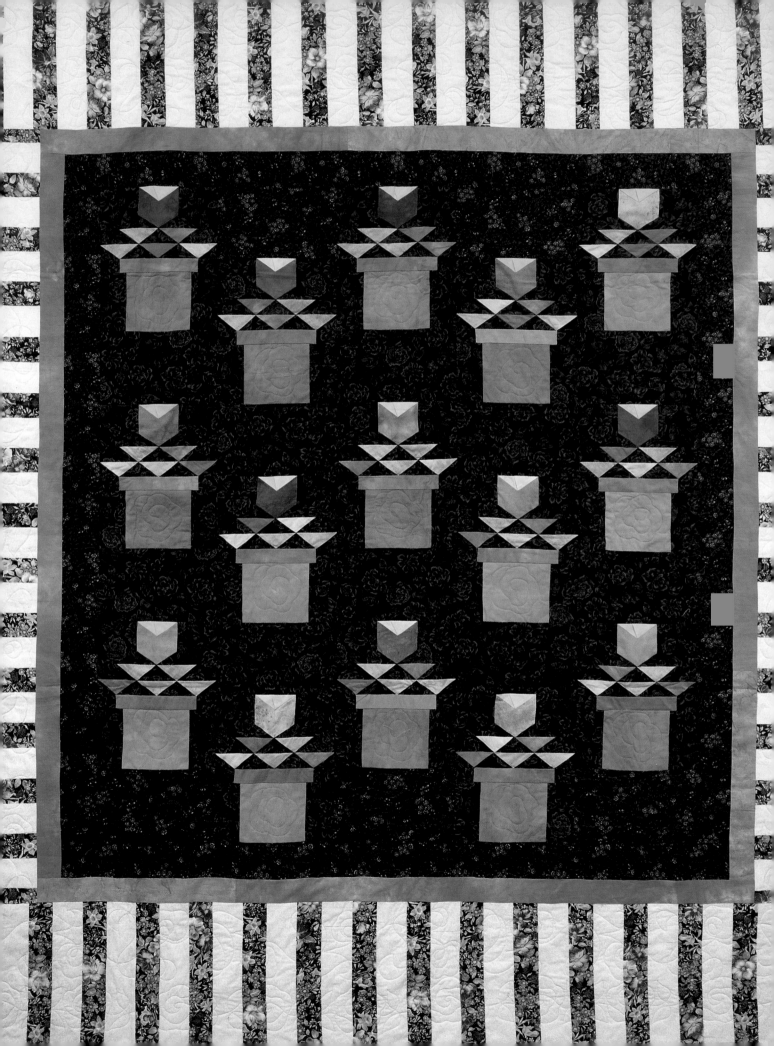

Paper-Piecing Primer

Understanding the Pattern Markings

THE PATTERNS for all the blocks in this book are actual size. (Patterns given for the project "Wedge Log Cabin" are for a queen-size quilt; you'll need to enlarge or reduce them for a king- or twin-size quilt.) The patterns are found on pages 60–76.

As you look at each pattern, you'll notice that each section is numbered. The numbers indicate the sewing sequence for the fabric pieces. Second, each pattern has solid lines around its outer edges, which indicate the finished size of the block. Seam allowances aren't included, so you will need to allow enough fabric beyond the pattern edges for seam allowances. If you prefer, you can add a ¼" seam allowance to your foundations when you copy the patterns. All the other lines on the patterns are sewing lines, along which you'll stitch your fabric pieces to the paper.

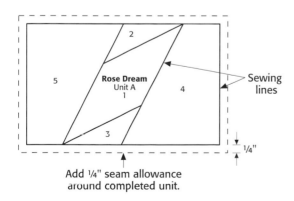

Add ¼" seam allowance around completed unit.

You'll also notice that nearly all of the blocks are made up of two or more paper-pieced units. Sometimes you just can't stitch all the pieces for the block together into one big section due to seam intersections. So, blocks are broken down into smaller units that can be paper pieced easily. Then the paper-pieced units are sewn together to complete the block. You'll find instructions for sewing the block units together in the project directions.

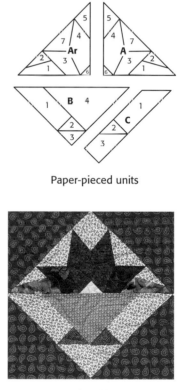

Paper-pieced units

Finished block

Finally, you'll notice that some patterns are the mirror image of the block you see in the photo. This is because the blocks are sewn from the marked side of the paper foundation, which is the wrong side of the finished patchwork block. For symmetrical blocks the patterns and finished blocks look exactly the same, but for asymmetrical blocks the finished blocks are mirror images of the printed patterns. It may look confusing at first, but I guarantee you'll get the hang of it as soon as you stitch your first block.

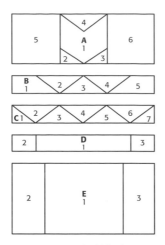

Symmetrical block

Finished block

Selecting a Foundation Material

BLOCK PATTERNS for foundation piecing are transferred to foundations—the paper or fabric on which you stitch your fabrics. The foundations provide sewing lines as well as stability for sewing and piecing blocks together. They can be either permanent or temporary, depending upon the desired result and whether you plan to quilt by hand or by machine.

Permanent foundations, of fabric or interfacing, remain in the completed quilt, adding an extra layer. I prefer to use paper foundations, which you remove before completing the quilt so they don't add bulk. Many types of paper can be used for foundations. Cheap tracing paper is a good choice. It's easy to see the fabrics through the paper—a huge benefit when placing fabric pieces—and it's inexpensive. Vellum is also transparent, but it's a bit more expensive. Just be aware that not all types of paper can be run through a photocopy machine. That Patchwork Place produces Papers for Foundation Piecing, which is great for paper piecing and works great in a photocopy machine or laser printer.

BAKER'S SECRET

✳

Parchment paper for baking is a great choice for foundations. It's made to withstand the heat of an oven, so it's quite safe for pressing with your iron as you add fabrics to it and need to press the seams. It can be found in the baking aisle of your grocery store. It comes on a roll, usually in either white (bleached) or natural (unbleached). It's not totally see-through, but it's not opaque, either. Another benefit is that it's quite easy to tear away once your project is complete.

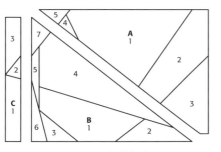

Asymmetrical block

Finished block

Transferring the Patterns

TO REPRODUCE the patterns, trace or photocopy them from this book onto your foundation paper. When tracing, use a ruler to ensure accuracy. Be sure to copy the piecing sequence numbers as well as the pattern lines. If you prefer to include ¼" seam allowances on your patterns, use a ruler to mark them on the foundations, too.

If you choose to photocopy the patterns, watch out for distortion. To test the precision of the photocopier, make one copy of the block and measure it to be sure the size matches that of the original. Some photocopiers distort in one direction only, so measure both vertically and horizontally.

Once you finish copying the patterns, cut them apart outside the marked lines.

Enlarging or Reducing Blocks

IT IS EASY TO enlarge or reduce the patterns to create blocks of any size you desire. Simply use a copy machine with enlarging and reducing capabilities. But remember that when you enlarge or reduce, your seam allowances will get larger or smaller, too. Instead of running off a bunch of larger or smaller copies, experiment until you get a copy on which the block is the desired size. Then redraw the seam allowances on this copy so that they measure ¼". Use this as your pattern to trace or photocopy additional blocks at 100 percent.

Precutting the Block Fabrics

UNLIKE TRADITIONAL piecing, where patches of fabric are cut precisely for accurate assembly, in paper piecing, patches are cut oversized. Simply cut the fabric into a chunk at least ½" larger all around than the area it will fill. The excess fabric will be trimmed away after you stitch the next piece of fabric in the sequence. I have

COLOR-CODED PATTERNS

✳

Color-code or mark your patterns so that you stitch the correct fabric in the proper place in your block. When making multiple blocks, I make an extra copy of the pattern, color-code it, and use it as a key so I can easily see where the different fabrics go. You can also mark your actual paper foundations. For instance, on the paper foundation for the Potted Posies block, I add a *P* for the pink flower, a *G* for the green leaves, and a *B* for the brown pot. I leave the background pieces unmarked.

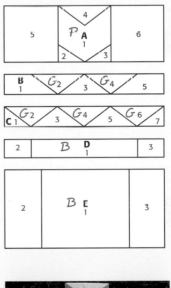

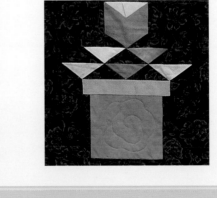

provided cutting charts with each project that show how large I rough cut my fabrics for piecing. I suggest that you make a sample block to be sure you're comfortable with how large the pieces are cut before you cut all your fabric. Some paper-piecers like to have a larger allowance for safety, while others like to minimize fabric waste.

One of the beauties of foundation piecing is that the foundation stabilizes the fabrics, and as a result it is unnecessary to follow grain-line rules strictly when cutting fabric. In normal template or rotary cutting, it is imperative that edges are cut on the straight of grain; if they are cut on the bias the unstable pieces will stretch and cause problems when they are pieced together. There is one important point to remember, however, with paper piecing: Leave your foundations in place until you sew your blocks together so that the fabrics don't stretch.

Preparing to Sew

SET YOUR SEWING machine for a stitch length of eighteen to twenty stitches per inch. The short stitch length creates a stronger stitch that won't break when you tear the paper away, and the closely spaced perforations also facilitate removal of the paper.

Choose your thread according to the fabrics selected. Gray is a good choice for most fabrics, while a light beige or even white may work best for light fabrics.

Basic Paper Piecing

THE FOLLOWING is a step-by-step overview for paper piecing a block.

1. Trace or photocopy the block pattern onto your foundation paper.

2. Cut fabric for all the pieces used in the block, each piece at least ½" larger on all sides than the area it is to cover.

3. Place piece 1 on the unmarked side of the foundation with the wrong side of the fabric facing the paper. If you wish, use a small dab of fabric glue-stick to hold the fabric to the paper.

4. With right sides together, place piece 2 against piece 1 so that the majority of piece 2 is over area 1. Leave about ½" of fabric extending into the area marked 2. Working from the marked side of the foundation, stitch along the seam line between area 1 and area 2. Begin and end the stitching several stitches beyond the ends of the line.

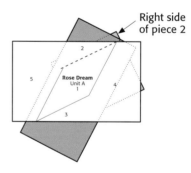

5. Flip up piece 2 to be sure it covers the area marked 2 in the pattern when it is pressed into place. Then trim the seam allowance to ¼".

6. Fold piece 2 over the seam and press it in place.

7. Add the remaining pieces in numerical order in the same manner.

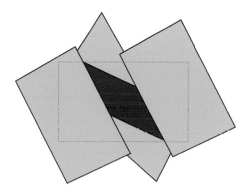

8. Lay the block, fabric side down (marked paper foundation up), on a cutting mat. Using a rotary cutter and ruler, trim the edges of the block ¼" outside the marked lines to allow for a seam allowance around the block. Make sure you cut through the paper foundation and the fabric.

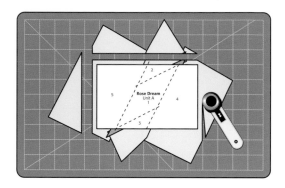

9. To join units into a completed block, refer to the individual project directions. Units are usually joined in alphabetical order, although sometimes unit A is joined to unit B, unit C is joined to unit D, and then the two larger units are sewn together. When sewing units together, be sure to stitch along the solid line.

10. If you made your foundations with seam allowances, remove the paper in the seam allowances only. Press the seam allowances open, unless the project directions specify otherwise.

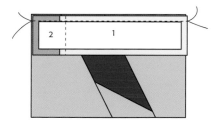

A PERFECT MATCH

※

For a perfect match every time, use pins to help you match the seams of your units. With two units placed right sides together and working from the paper side of the top unit, poke a pin into the corner of the stitching line at one end of the seam you are matching.

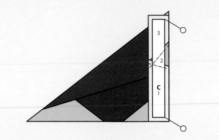

Hold the pieces together as you poke another pin into the bottom piece to make sure it is coming out at exactly the corner point of the bottom unit. It may take a few tries, but by peeking underneath you'll get the point exactly.

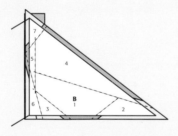

Pinch the units together, matching the raw edges along the seam. Use a pin or two to hold the pieces together. Remove the first corner-matching pin and sew the seam, removing other pins as you approach them.

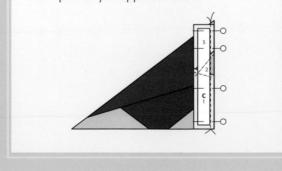

MORE TIPS FOR PAPER-PIECING SUCCESS

※

- Although I usually use my ¼" presser foot for all quilt-related sewing, you may find that an open-toe foot helps you see the line as you sew.
- Leave the paper foundations in place until after the quilt top is completed. Blocks are easier to align this way and will not become distorted by the tearing process. Also, do not worry about the grain line of the block edges. The paper foundations stabilize the edges throughout the construction process.
- When pressing, use a hot, dry iron so that you don't distort your blocks.
- To avoid distorting the paper foundation or transferring ink from the paper foundation onto your iron or fabric, press only on the fabric side of the blocks, and use a press cloth underneath to protect your ironing-board cover.

The V Technique for Inset Pieces

I'M ALWAYS on the lookout for an easier way to do things, so for the "Poinsettia Baskets" and "Potted Posies" quilts I adapted a technique that eliminates a unit. I call it the V technique. In "Potted Posies," for instance, I stitched the yellow flower centers with the V technique, then folded back the fabric, forming what looks like a prairie point. The technique wouldn't work for all situations, but for these two quilts the added dimension it gives works nicely.

1. Refer to "Basic Paper Piecing" on page 12 to stitch pieces 1 through 5 on the Potted Posies block. With the right side of the background fabric facing the right sides of the flower fabrics, stitch a large piece of background fabric to the V-shaped seam. Trim the seam allowance.

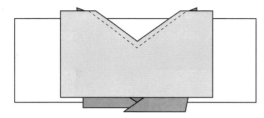

2. Fold one side of the background fabric up along the stitching.

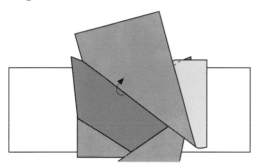

3. Fold up the other side, so it looks like a folded prairie point. Pin the fabric in place, then baste along the edge to hold it.

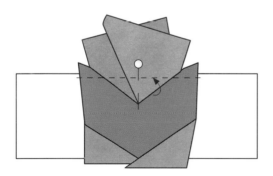

4. Complete the rest of the block, following the project instructions. When the quilt top is assembled, remove any basting stitches that show.

Finishing the Quilt

ONCE YOUR blocks and any border units are paper pieced, quilt-top assembly is just about the same as for any other type of patchwork quilt. Except that you have to remove the papers before you can quilt it!

Assembling the Quilt Top

1. Refer to the layout diagram for the quilt to arrange the finished blocks and any other required fabric pieces in the proper order. Sew the blocks together along the outer solid lines on the foundations in the order indicated in the project instructions. After each seam is stitched, remove the foundation paper *from the seam allowance only* (if you made foundations that include seam allowances). To do so, gently tear the paper as if you were tearing stamps apart. A gentle tug against the seam will give you a head start in loosening the paper foundation from the stitching. Press the seam allowances in the direction specified for each project.

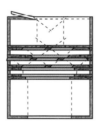

NO-PIN "PINNING"

✳

Using your fine sewing pins for paper piecing can take a toll on them, dulling or bending them as they go through layers of paper and fabrics. Instead, I like to use vinyl-coated paper clips to hold my fabric pieces together for stitching, as long as there are no critical matching points that need to be aligned.

2. After the individual rows are made, stitch the rows together in the same manner, following the layout diagram for the project.

3. Remove the remaining paper foundations from the backs of the blocks.

4. Press the completed quilt top gently. Lift the iron up and down, rather than dragging it, so as not to distort the blocks.

Preparing for Quilting

I have included quilting suggestions and the names of the designs I used in the project directions for each of the quilts in this book, although you should feel free to use whatever quilting design you prefer.

1. Mark the quilt top with the desired quilting design, if necessary.

2. Cut the batting and backing fabric 8" larger than the quilt top. This will give you 4" extra on each side of the quilt, which is the minimum allowance a long-arm quilter requires.

3. Lay the backing, wrong side up, on a flat surface. Place the batting over the backing. Center the quilt top, right side up, on top of the batting and backing. Working from the center out, baste the three layers of the quilt "sandwich" together with thread, safety pins, or a quilt tacking gun. If you prefer to use a basting spray, spray the layers as you add them. If you plan to have your quilt quilted on a long-arm quilting machine, do not baste.

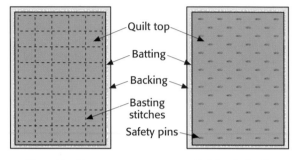

Thread basting   Safety-pin basting

4. Quilt the top as indicated in the project directions or as you desire. The quilts shown in this book have all been quilted on long-arm quilting machines. The names of the patterns used are provided if you'd like to duplicate the look. If you haven't used the services of a professional quilter, you may be surprised to learn that not all the designs they're using are allover patterns. A few of the designs I used are shown below.

5. When you are finished quilting, remove all basting stitches, quilt tacks, or any remaining safety pins. If you've used a basting spray, you may want to wash your quilt after it's bound to remove any adhesive residues.

Making and Applying Binding

For binding all of the quilts in this book, I used 2¼" strips cut on the straight grain of the fabric. The only time I use bias binding is on curved edges. If you prefer to use bias binding, be sure to purchase extra fabric.

1. For straight-grain binding, simply cut strips from the lengthwise or crosswise grain of the fabric. Join the ends of the strips together to make one long, continuous strip.

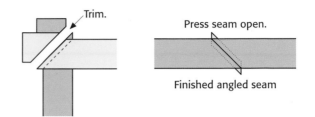

Trim.

Press seam open.

Finished angled seam

2. With wrong sides together, press the binding strip in half lengthwise.

3. Trim the batting and backing fabric even with the raw edges of the quilt.

4. Place the binding strip along one edge of the quilt, right sides together and matching raw edges. Leaving the first 6" or so of the binding free, stitch the binding to the quilt, using a ¼" seam allowance. Stop stitching ¼" from the corner. Backstitch and remove the quilt from the machine.

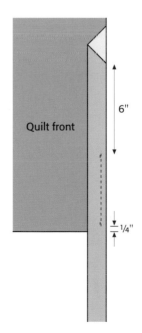

6"

Quilt front

¼"

5. Turn the quilt to prepare to sew the next edge. To miter the corner, fold the binding straight up, creating a 45°-angle fold.

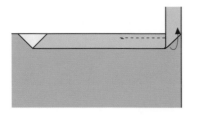

6. Fold the binding down so the fold is even with the top edge of the quilt and the raw edges of the binding are aligned with the raw edge of the quilt. Beginning at the edge, stitch the binding to the quilt, using a ¼" seam allowance and stopping ¼" from the next corner. Backstitch and remove the quilt from the machine. Continue the folding and stitching process for the remaining corners.

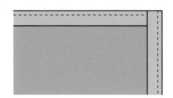

7. When you are within approximately 8" of the starting point, stop stitching. Bring the two ends of the binding together, and mark where they meet with pins. Clip the binding raw edges at the pin marks, being careful not to cut past the seam allowance or into the quilt layers.

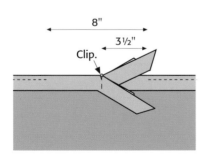

8. Open up the binding and match the ends as shown. Stitch the ends together with a diagonal seam.

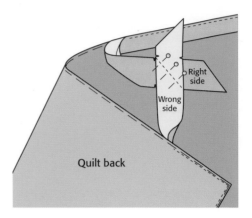

9. Refold the binding and check to be sure that the binding fits the quilt. Adjust the seam if necessary. Trim off the excess binding, press the seam allowance open, refold the binding, and finish stitching the binding to the edge.

10. Fold the binding to the back of the quilt, over the raw edges and covering the machine stitching. Slipstitch the binding in place by hand, mitering the corners as you go.

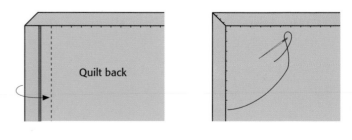

Rose Dream

Designed by Jodie Davis, 2001, Canton, Georgia, 84" x 96". Pieced by Janet Peterson, quilted by Karen Williams.

WHAT LITTLE *girl wouldn't love to drift off to sleep under this sweetheart of a quilt? Change the look by selecting any other two-color scheme, or make a totally scrappy rendition by piecing each block with different colors. I straightened out the lines on the traditional Rose Dream block, which is pieced with curved seams, making it super easy to paper piece in any colorway.*

****

Quilt Sizes

	Twin	Queen	King
Finished quilt size	72" x 84"	84" x 96"	108" x 96"
Finished block size	12" x 12"	12" x 12"	12" x 12"
Number of blocks	20	30	42

Materials *Yardages are based on 42"-wide fabric.*

	Twin	Queen	King
Assorted red, pink, and white, totaling	6½ yds.	8¾ yds.	11 yds.
Red #1 for first border	⅝ yd.	⅝ yd.	¾ yd.
Red #2 for third border	⅝ yd.	¾ yd.	⅞ yd.
Backing	5¼ yds.	7¾ yds.	8¾ yds.
Batting	80" x 92"	92" x 104"	116" x 104"
Binding	¾ yd.	¾ yd.	1 yd.

Cutting for Paper Piecing

TO MAKE paper piecing quicker and to minimize fabric waste, precut your fabrics for the paper-pieced units. Since some paper-piecers like to have more leeway with their fabric than others, make a sample block to determine if these measurements work for you before you cut all your fabric.

Piece	Size to Rough Cut
Unit A, piece 1	2½" x 6"
Unit A, pieces 2 and 3	1¾" x 3¾"
Unit A, pieces 4 and 5	3¾" x 5½"
Unit B, piece 1	2¼" x 5¾"
Unit B, piece 2	2" x 2¼"

Additional Cutting

Fabric	Used For	Size to Cut	Number to Cut		
			Twin	Queen	King
Red #1	First border	2" x 42"	8	8	9
Assorted reds, pinks, and whites	Second border	3½" x 3½"	80	96	110
Red #2	Third border	2" x 42"	8	9	10
Assorted reds, pinks, and whites	Fourth border	6½" x 6½"	48	56	64

Piecing the Quilt Top

1. Refer to "Transferring the Patterns" on page 11 to prepare the foundations for your blocks. Each block is made up of 4 quarter-blocks, each of those consisting of 1 A unit and 2 B units. The foundation patterns are on page 60. You'll need to make the following numbers of foundations, according to the size of the quilt you're making:

	Twin	Queen	King
Unit A	80	120	168
Unit B	160	240	336

2. Cut the fabrics as indicated in the cutting charts.

3. Referring to "Basic Paper Piecing" on page 12, piece the units. Stitch a B unit to the top and bottom of a matching A unit to make a quarter-block.

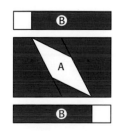

Make 4 quarter-blocks
per block.

4. Stitch 4 quarter-blocks together, as shown, to make a block. Repeat to make the total number of blocks needed for your quilt.

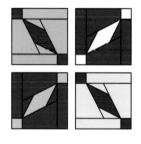

5. Referring to the quilt layout diagram, arrange the blocks in rows. The twin-size quilt has 5 rows of 4 blocks each, the queen-size has 6 rows of 5 blocks each, and the king-size has 6 rows of 7 blocks each.

When you are pleased with the arrangement, sew the blocks together into rows. Remove the paper from the seam allowances and press the seams in one direction. Sew the rows together. Remove the paper from the seam allowances. Press the seams in one direction.

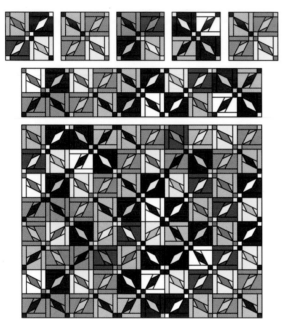

Quilt Layout

Borders

THIS QUILT has 4 borders. The first border is narrow and unpieced, the second border is pieced with small squares, the third border is narrow and unpieced, and the fourth border is pieced with large squares.

1. To make the first border, sew the red #1 strips together end to end in pairs. Measure the length of the quilt top, and cut 2 of the joined strips to that measurement. Stitch the strips to the sides of the quilt top, and press the seam allowances toward the borders.

2. Measure the width of the quilt top, including the borders you've just added. Cut the remaining 2 joined strips to that measurement. Stitch the strips to the top and bottom of the quilt top, and press the seam allowances toward the borders.

3. To make the second border, sew the 3½" squares into strips, as shown below. Press the seam allowances in one direction.

	Twin	Queen	King
Side borders	21 squares	25 squares	25 squares
Top and bottom borders	19 squares	23 squares	31 squares

4. Sew the side borders to the quilt top. Press the seam allowances toward the first border. Repeat for the top and bottom borders.

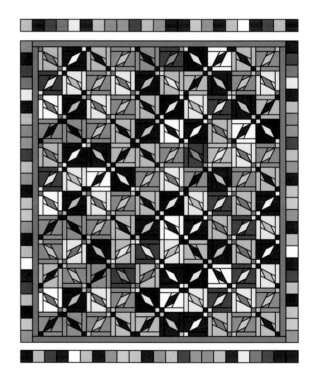

5. To make the third border, sew the red #2 strips together end to end in pairs. Measure the length of the quilt top, and cut 2 of the joined strips to that measurement. Stitch the strips to the sides of the quilt top, and press the seam allowances toward the third border.

6. Measure the width of the quilt top, including the borders you've just added. Cut the remaining 2 joined strips to that measurement. Stitch the strips to the top and bottom of the quilt top, and press the seam allowances toward the third border.

7. To make the fourth border, sew the 6½" squares into sets, as shown below. Press the seam allowances in one direction.

	Twin	Queen	King
Side borders	12 squares	14 squares	14 squares
Top and bottom borders	12 squares	14 squares	18 squares

8. Sew the side borders to the quilt top. Press the seam allowances toward the third border. Repeat for the top and bottom borders.

Finishing the Quilt

1. Remove the remaining paper foundations

2. Referring to "Preparing for Quilting" on page 16, layer the quilt top, batting, and backing. Hand or machine quilt as desired. The center portion of the quilt shown was quilted with an allover 4½" scallop design, and a double feather design was used in the outer pieced border (see "Resources" on page 77).

3. Trim the excess batting and backing from your quilt, and bind the edges following the instructions in "Making and Applying Binding" on page 17.

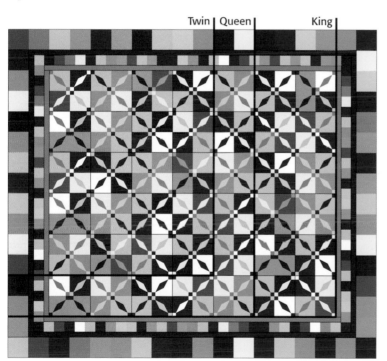

Poinsettia Baskets

Designed and pieced by Jodie Davis, 2001, Canton, Georgia, 84" x 98". Quilted by Sue Hunston.

D ECORATE YOUR *bedroom for the holidays with this sensational seasonal quilt. Or change the color scheme and create a different type of bloom by using pastels, summer brights, or even scraps of various colors for a multiflower quilt. Whatever your color choices, you'll find the blocks are quick and easy to piece because they have such large patches.*

✳·✳·✳

Quilt Sizes

	Twin	Queen	King
Finished quilt size	70" x 84"	84" x 98"	98" x 98"
Finished block size	9⅞" x 9⅞"	9⅞" x 9⅞"	9⅞" x 9⅞"
Number of pieced blocks	6	12	16
Number of pieced half-blocks for borders	14	18	20

Materials *Yardages are based on 42"-wide fabric.*

	Twin	Queen	King
Red #1 for flowers	1 yd.	1¼ yds.	1½ yds.
Red #2 for flowers	½ yd.	¾ yd.	1 yd.
Green for leaves	¾ yd.	1 yd.	1¼ yds.
Yellow for flowers	Scraps	Scraps	Scraps
Gold print for baskets and inner and outer borders	2¾ yds.	3¾ yds.	4½ yds.
Tan for basket feet	⅛ yd.	¼ yd.	¼ yd.
Light red print for basket backgrounds	2 yds.	3 yds.	4 yds.
Red for setting squares and triangles	1⅜ yds.	1⅜ yds.	1⅜ yds.
Large-scale red floral print for borders	1⅜ yds.	1⅜ yds.	1¾ yds.
Backing	5¼ yds.	7¾ yds.	9 yds.
Batting	78" x 92"	92" x 106"	106" x 106"
Binding	¾ yd.	⅞ yd.	1 yd.

Cutting for Paper Piecing

TO MAKE paper piecing quicker and to minimize fabric waste, precut the fabrics for the paper-pieced units. Since some paper-piecers like to have more leeway with their fabric than others, make a sample block to determine if these measurements work for you before you cut all your fabric.

Piece	Size to Rough Cut
Unit A, pieces 1 and 2	2½" x 42" strips
Unit A, piece 3	3" x 42" strips
Unit A, pieces 4 and 5	3½" x 42" strips
Unit A, piece 6	2" x 42" strips
Unit A, piece 7	6" x 42" strips
Unit B, pieces 1, 2, and 3	3" x 42" strips
Unit B, piece 4	7" x 42" strips
Unit C, pieces 1 and 2	2½" x 42" strips
Unit C, piece 3	4" x 42" strips
Unit C, piece 4	5½" x 42" strips
Unit D	7" x 42" strips

Additional Cutting

Fabric	Used For	Size to Cut	Number to Cut Twin	Queen	King
Red	Setting squares	10" x 10"	8	16	21
Red	Side setting triangles	14⅛" x 14⅛" ⊠	1 square	2 squares	2 squares
Red	Corner setting triangles	21⅞" x 21⅞" ◱	2 squares	2 squares	2 squares
Gold print	Side inner borders		Two 4" x 56½"	Two 4" x 70½"	Two 4" x 70½"
Gold print	Top and bottom inner borders		Two 4" x 49½"	Two 4" x 63½"	Two 4" x 77½"
Gold print	Side outer borders		Two 4" x 77½"	Two 4" x 91½"	Two 4" x 91½"
Gold print	Top and bottom outer borders		Two 4" x 70½"	Two 4" x 84½"	Two 4" x 98½"
Gold print	Middle border corners	3⅞" x 3⅞" ◱	4 squares	4 squares	4 squares
Large-scale red floral print	Middle border triangles	14⅛" x 14⅛" ⊠	3 squares	4 squares	5 squares

Additional Cutting (continued)

Fabric	Used For	Size to Cut	Twin	Queen	King
				Number to Cut	
Large-scale red floral print	Middle border corners	5⅞" x 5⅞" ◺	4 squares	4 squares	4 squares
Large-scale red floral print	Middle border corners	Piece E	4	4	4
Large-scale red floral print	Middle border corners	Piece E reverse	4	4	4

◺ = Cut squares diagonally once

⊠ = Cut squares diagonally twice

Piecing the Quilt Top

1. Refer to "Transferring the Patterns" on page 11 to prepare foundations for your blocks. Each Poinsettia Baskets block is made up of 4 paper-pieced units (A–D), which are stitched together before they are joined to complete the block. You'll need to make 6 copies of each pattern for a twin-size quilt, 12 of each for a queen-size quilt, or 16 of each for a king-size quilt. In addition, you'll need to make 14, 18, or 22, respectively, of units A and B for the middle border. The foundation patterns are on pages 61–63.

2. Cut the fabrics as indicated in the cutting charts.

3. Refer to "Basic Paper Piecing" on page 12 to construct the Poinsettia Baskets blocks and half-blocks for the middle border. To set in the background piece for the flower parts of the blocks, see "The V Technique for Inset Pieces" on page 14.

4. When you have completed all the A, B, and C units, stitch the A and A reverse units together in pairs and the B units to the C units. Then stitch the flower half-blocks to the basket half-blocks to complete the number of blocks required for your quilt. Set aside the remaining pairs of A and A reverse flower units.

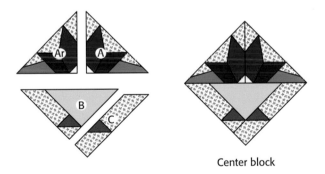

Center block

5. Referring to the quilt layout diagram on page 28, arrange the pieced blocks, setting squares, and side setting triangles in rows. Stitch them together in diagonal rows. Remove paper from the seam allowances and press the seam allowances toward the setting squares and triangles. Stitch the rows together. Remove paper from the seam allowances and press the seam allowances toward the plain fabrics.

6. Sew the corner setting triangles to the quilt and press the seams toward the triangles.

Twin | Queen | King

Quilt Layout

Borders

THE GOLD inner border is attached to the pieced middle border before being attached to the quilt top. Then the pieced corner blocks are attached, and finally the gold outer border is sewn to the quilt.

1. To make the pieced middle border, lay out the pieced half-blocks and the large-scale red floral print triangles as indicated in the illustration below. (Reserve 4 pieced half-blocks for the corners.) Stitch the half-blocks and the triangles together to make 4 borders. Sew a red floral print triangle to the end of each border. Remove the paper from the seam allowances, and press the seam allowances toward the plain triangles.

2. Attach the gold inner border strips to the middle border by sewing them to the large-scale red floral print triangles.

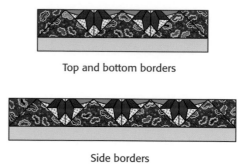

Top and bottom borders

Side borders

3. To make the 4 corner blocks, sew a gold 3⅞" triangle to each red-print piece E and piece E reverse to create 8 pieced triangles. Sew the triangles together in pairs as shown, to make 4 large triangles. Sew a pieced half-block to each of the large triangles to complete the corner blocks.

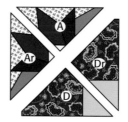

Corner block
Make 4.

4. Attach the side borders to the quilt, by sewing the gold inner borders to the sides of the quilt. Press the seam allowances toward the inner borders.

5. Stitch the corner blocks to the ends of the top and bottom borders, making sure that the gold triangles match up with the gold inner borders. Attach the top and bottom borders to the quilt, by sewing the gold inner border fabric to the top and bottom of the quilt. Press the seam allowances toward the gold fabric.

6. Stitch the gold outer borders to the sides of the quilt top. Press the seam allowances toward the gold borders. Repeat for the top and bottom borders.

Twin

Queen

King

Finishing the Quilt

1. Remove the remaining paper foundations from the backs of the blocks.

2. Referring to "Preparing for Quilting" on page 16, layer the quilt top, batting, and backing. Hand or machine quilt as desired. The quilt shown was quilted on a long-arm quilting machine using the Folk Lily pattern (see "Resources" on page 77).

3. Trim the excess batting and backing from your quilt, and bind the edges following the instructions in "Making and Applying Binding" on page 17.

Spinning Wheels

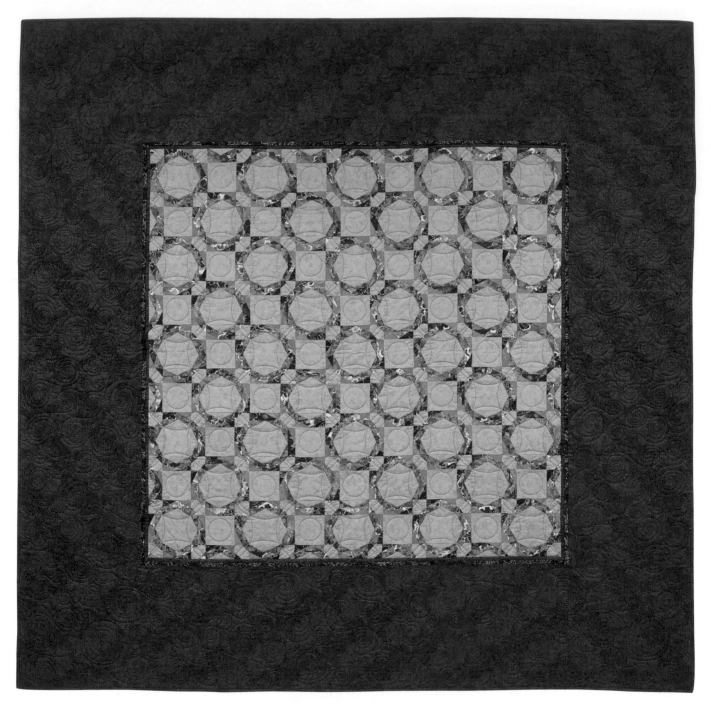

Designed and pieced by Jodie Davis, 2001, Canton, Georgia, 92" x 92". Quilted by Sue Hunston.

THE INSPIRATION *for this quilt came from two large-scale multicolored prints. They made me say "I've gotta make a quilt from these fabrics" the minute I saw them. This is a fun project to make no matter what your fabric selections. It's amazing how all those straight lines and angles turn into a circular design that's full of motion once the units are stitched together.*

✳✳✳

Quilt Sizes

	Twin	Queen	King
Finished quilt size	80" x 92"	92" x 92"	104" x 104"
Number of pieced rectangle A units	284	360	358
Number of pieced square B units	80	100	144
Number of plain squares	63	81	121

Materials *Yardages are based on 42"-wide fabric.*

	Twin	Queen	King
Light teal for backgrounds	2¾ yds.	3¼ yds.	4¾ yds.
Green hand-dyed	¾ yd.	1 yd.	2 yds.
Fuchsia batik for piecing and piping border	1¾ yds.	1¾ yds.	2¼ yds.
Multi print	1½ yds.	2¾ yds.	2¾ yds.
Royal blue print	1¼ yds.	2 yds.	3¾ yds.
Purple print for borders	4 yds.	4½ yds.	5 yds.
Backing	7½ yds.	8½ yds.	9½ yds.
Batting	88" x 100"	100" x 100"	112" x 112"
Binding	⅞ yd.	1 yd.	1 yd.

Cutting for Paper Piecing

To MAKE paper piecing quicker and to minimize fabric waste, precut your fabrics for the paper-pieced units. Since some paper-piecers like to have more leeway with their fabric than others, make a sample block to determine if these measurements work for you before you cut all your fabric.

Piece	Size to Rough Cut
Unit A, pieces 1, 2, and 3	2" x 42" strips
Unit B, piece 1	3" x 42" strips
Unit B, pieces 2 and 3	1¾" x 42" strips

Additional Cutting

			Number to Cut		
Fabric	Used For	Size to Cut	Twin	Queen	King
Light teal	Background	4½" x 42"	8 strips; from them cut 63 squares, 4½" x 4½"	11 strips; from them cut 81 squares, 4½" x 4½"	16 strips; from them cut 121 squares, 4½" x 4½"
Purple print	Inner border	1½"-wide strips, cut on lengthwise grain	2 strips, each 46½" long; 2 strips, each 56½" long	2 strips, each 56½" long; 2 strips, each 58½" long	2 strips, each 68½" long; 2 strips, each 70½" long
Purple print	Outer border	17½"-wide strips, cut on lengthwise grain	2 strips, each 46½" long; 2 strips, each 58½" long	4 strips, each 58½" long	4 strips, each 70½" long
Purple print	Outer border corners	17½" x 17½"	4	4	4
Fuchsia batik	Piping border	1½"-wide strips, cut on lengthwise grain	2 strips, each 46½" long; 2 strips, each 58½" long	4 strips, each 58½" long	4 strips, each 70½" long

Piecing the Quilt Top

1. Refer to "Transferring the Patterns" on page 11 to prepare foundations for your blocks. The foundation patterns are on page 63. You'll need to make the following numbers of foundations, according to the size of the quilt you're making:

	Twin	Queen	King
Unit A	284	360	528
Unit B	80	100	144

2. Cut the fabrics as indicated in the cutting charts.

3. Referring to "Basic Paper Piecing" on page 12, construct the A and B units. To form the interlocking circle pattern in the quilt, you'll need to piece half of the A units using royal blue fabric. The remaining A units are made half in one colorway and half in another, as shown. All the B units are pieced with the same fabrics in the same places.

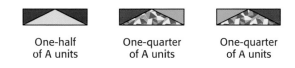

One-half   One-quarter   One-quarter
of A units   of A units   of A units

B unit

4. Sew the A units together in pairs, with the light teal unit on the bottom of the pair, as shown.

Sew A units into pairs.

5. Arrange the pieced units and the plain light-teal squares as shown in the quilt layout diagram. Be careful when placing the pieced units, as they don't all face in the same direction. If you rotate any of the pieces when you're assembling the quilt, your finished quilt won't have the interlocking circular design. Stitch the pieces together into rows and then stitch the rows together. Remove the paper from the seam allowances and press them to one side as you go.

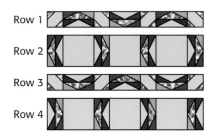

Repeat rows 1–4 according to quilt size.

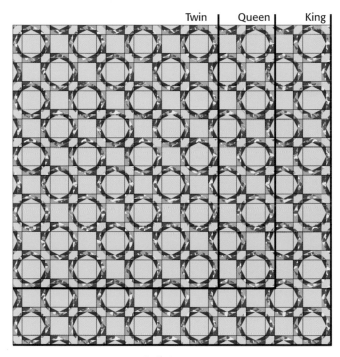

Quilt Layout

Borders

1. Stitch the purple inner borders to the sides of the quilt. Press the seam allowances toward the borders.

2. Stitch the remaining purple inner borders to the top and bottom of the quilt. Press the seam allowances toward the borders.

3. To make the piping border, fold and press the fuchsia batik strips in half lengthwise, wrong sides together. Pin them to the edges of the quilt top, overlapping them at the corners as shown. Machine baste them in place using a scant ¼" seam allowance.

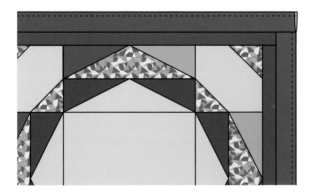

4. Stitch a purple outer border to each side of the quilt top. Press the seam allowances toward the outer border.

5. Stitch a purple outer border corner square to each end of the 2 remaining purple outer border pieces. Press the seam allowances toward the long border pieces. Stitch the borders to the top and bottom of the quilt, matching the seams with the border seams on the quilt top.

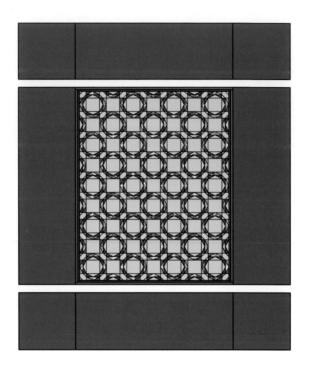

Finishing the Quilt

1. Remove the remaining paper foundations.

2. Referring to "Preparing for Quilting" on page 16, layer the quilt top, batting, and backing. Hand or machine quilt as desired. The paper-pieced portion of the quilt shown was quilted with a series of 3 concentric circles using Circle-Ease (see "Resources" on page 77). For the wide border, an attractive free-hand design of various-size swirls was machine quilted.

3. Trim the excess batting and backing from your quilt, and bind the edges following the instructions in "Making and Applying Binding" on page 17.

Dancing Ribbon Stars

Designed by Jodie Davis, 2001, Canton, Georgia, 78" x 90". Pieced by Michele Bautsch, quilted by Karen Williams.

W ITH ITS *lively pattern of ribbons cavorting across the quilt top, this design is full of energy. The large print in the outer border inspired my color choices, and I chose a coordinating leaf print for the background fabric to add bursts of color across the quilt. A more subtle print or solid fabric in the background would make the swirling ribbon design more prominent—the choice is yours!*

⁕⁕⁕

Quilt Sizes

	Twin	Queen	King
Finished quilt size	78" x 90"	90" x 102"	102" x 102"
Finished block size	12" x 12"	12" x 12"	12" x 12"
Number of blocks	30	42	49

Materials *Yardages are based on 42"-wide fabric.*

	Twin	Queen	King
Peach batik	1¾ yds.	2 yds.	2¼ yds.
Pink batik	1¾ yds.	2 yds.	2¼ yds.
Green batik	4 yds.	5¼ yds.	6 yds.
Yellow print for block background	5¾ yds.	8 yds.	9 yds.
Pink-and-green stripe for inner border	1⅛ yds.	1¼ yds.	1½ yds.
Large floral print for outer border	1¾ yds.	2¼ yds.	2½ yds.
Backing	7¼ yds.	8¼ yds.	9¼ yds.
Batting	86" x 98"	98" x 110"	110" x 110"
Binding	¾ yd.	1 yd.	1 yd.

Cutting for Paper Piecing

TO MAKE paper piecing quicker and to minimize fabric waste, precut your fabrics for the paper-pieced units. Since some paper-piecers like to have more leeway with their fabric than others, make a sample block to determine if these measurements work for you before you cut all your fabric.

Piece	Size to Rough Cut
Units A–D and F, piece 1	4" x 42" strips
Units E and G, piece 1	7" x 42" strips
All other pieces	2¼" x 42" strips

Additional Cutting

Fabric	Used For	Size to Cut	Number to Cut		
			Twin	Queen	King
Pink-and-green stripe	Inner border	3½" x 42" strips; cut into 3½" x 6½" rectangles	4 strips; from them cut 22 rectangles	5 strips; from them cut 26 rectangles	5 strips; from them cut 28 rectangles

Piecing the Quilt Top

1. Refer to "Transferring the Patterns" on page 11 to prepare foundations for your blocks. Each block is made up of 12 paper-pieced sections (4 each of units A, B, C, and D), which are stitched together before they are joined to complete each block. Refer to the chart below for the number of each unit you need to prepare for the size of quilt you are making. The foundation patterns are on pages 64–66.

Unit	Twin	Queen	King
A	120	168	196
B	120	168	196
C	120	168	196
D	120	168	196
A reverse	48	56	60
E	22	26	28
E reverse	22	26	28
F	4	4	4
F reverse	4	4	4
G	4	4	4

2. Cut the fabrics as indicated in the cutting charts.

3. Refer to "Basic Paper Piecing" on page 12 to construct the A, B, C, and D units. For unit B, make half with pink batik in piece 2 and half with peach batik. For unit C, make half with pink in piece 3 and half with peach.

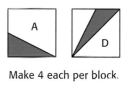

Make 4 each per block.

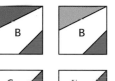

Make 2 each per block.

4. Referring to the block diagrams below, stitch 1 each of unit A, B, C, and D together to form a quarter of a block. Repeat to make 3 more quarter-blocks, following the color placement shown below.

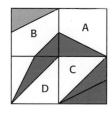 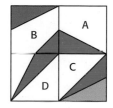

Make 2 per block.   Make 2 per block.

5. Arrange the 4 quarter-blocks, noticing that the units are stitched together in the same manner, but the quarter-blocks are rotated one-quarter turn as you work your way around the block. Stitch the 4 quarter-blocks together to complete 1 block. Repeat to make the number of blocks required for your size of quilt.

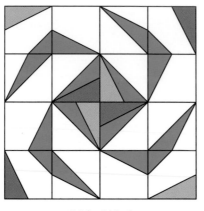

Finished block

6. Following the quilt layout diagram, arrange the blocks. Sew the blocks into rows. Remove the foundation papers from the seam allowances and press the seams in one row all in the same direction. Press seam allowances in opposite directions in alternating rows.

7. Stitch the rows together, and press the seam allowances all in one direction.

Quilt Layout

Borders

THE INNER border is made with the pink-and-green-stripe rectangles and pieced A reverse units. The outer border is made with units E, F, and G.

1. Piece the A reverse units, using the stripe fabric for piece 1 in all the units. For piece 2, use the pink batik for half the units, and the peach batik for the other half.

2. Referring to the quilt layout diagram for the size of your quilt, piece 4 inner borders, alternating the stripe rectangles and the A reverse units. Pay careful attention to the color placement and orientation of the A reverse units so that your pieced border will complete the star units in the quilt blocks. Remove the foundation papers and press the seam allowances toward the stripe rectangles.

Top and bottom borders
Make half pink and half peach.

Side borders
Make half pink and half peach.

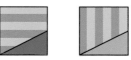

Corners
Make 2 pink and 2 peach.

Top and bottom borders

Side borders

3. Sew the 2 longer borders to the sides of the quilt. Press seam allowances toward the borders. Attach the remaining borders to the top and bottom of the quilt in the same manner and press.

4. Piece the E, E reverse, F, F reverse, and G units, referring to the block diagrams below for color placement.

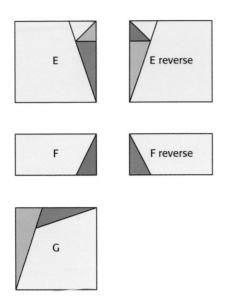

5. Referring to the diagrams below, piece the 4 outer borders, alternating the E and E reverse units. Attach an F and F reverse unit to the ends of each border, as shown below. Remove the foundation papers and press seams to one side.

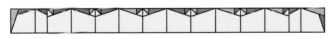

Top and bottom borders

Side borders

6. Sew the outer borders to the sides of the quilt. Press seam allowances toward the outer borders. Attach the G corner blocks to the remaining 2 borders, then stitch the borders to the top and bottom of the quilt. Press the seam allowances toward the outer borders.

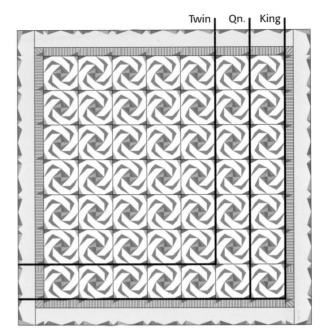

Finishing the Quilt

1. Remove the remaining paper foundations.

2. Referring to "Preparing for Quilting" on page 16, layer the quilt top, batting, and backing. Hand or machine quilt as desired. The quilt shown was quilted on a long-arm quilting machine in the Chantilly Lace pattern (see "Resources" on page 77).

3. Trim the excess batting and backing from your quilt, and bind the edges following the instructions in "Making and Applying Binding" on page 17.

Songbird Serenade

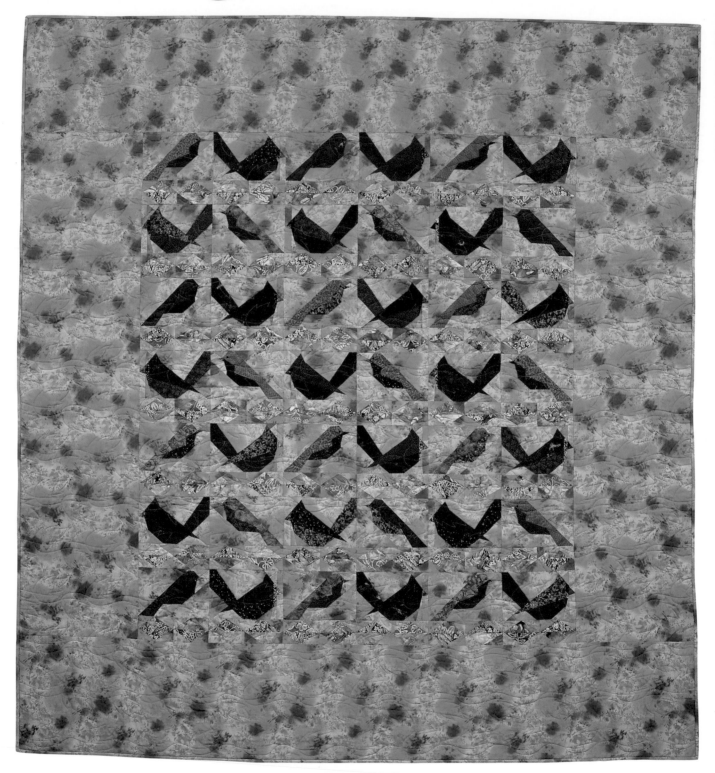

Designed by Jodie Davis, 2001, Canton, Georgia, 84" x 93". Pieced by Joann Spiers, quilted by Sylvia Davis.

_C_ARDINALS AND _bluebirds sing from their perches on this vibrant quilt. For a more subdued version, give your birds a woodsy setting by selecting a neutral coffee-colored print for the background.
If you've got a hefty fabric stash, mix up the reds and blues for your birds as I did, or you can change the
look by making all of them from the same fabrics._

✳✳✳

Quilt Sizes

	Twin	Queen	King
Finished quilt size	75" x 93"	84" x 93"	102" x 93"
Finished block size	9" x 9"	9" x 9"	9" x 9"
Number of Cardinal blocks	18	21	28
Number of Bluebird blocks	17	21	28

Materials _Yardages are based on 42"-wide fabric._

	Twin	Queen	King
Assorted red for cardinals, totaling	1 yd.	1¼ yds.	1½ yds.
Assorted blue for bluebirds, totaling	¾ yd.	1 yd.	1¼ yds.
Assorted orange/red for bluebird breasts, totaling	⅜ yd.	½ yd.	¾ yd.
Black for cardinals	4 strips, 2" x 42"	5 strips, 2" x 42"	6 strips, 2" x 42"
Brown for beaks	2 strips, 1½" x 42"	3 strips, 1½" x 42"	3 strips, 1½" x 42"
Assorted green for leaves, totaling	1½ yd.	2 yds.	2½ yds.
Background for pieced blocks	6½ yds.	8 yds.	10 yds.
Background for borders	4 yds.	4¼ yds.	4¾ yds.
Backing	7 yds.	7¾ yds.	8½ yds.
Batting	83" x 101"	92" x 101"	110" x 101"
Binding	¾ yd.	⅞ yd.	1 yd.
Embroidery floss or ¼" buttons for eyes			

Cutting for Paper Piecing

To MAKE paper piecing quicker and to minimize fabric waste, precut your fabrics for the paper-pieced units. Since some paper-piecers like to have more leeway with their fabric than others, make a sample block to determine if these measurements work for you before you cut all your fabric.

Piece	Fabric	Size to Rough Cut
Cardinal unit A, piece 1	Background	6" x 6"
Cardinal unit A, piece 2	Red #2	3" x 6½"
Cardinal unit A, piece 3	Background	3½" x 4½"
Cardinal unit A, piece 4	Red #1	2" x 1½"
Cardinal unit A, piece 5	Background	2" x 2"
Cardinal unit B, piece 1	Red #1	3" x 6½"
Cardinal unit B, piece 2	Background	2" x 5"
Cardinal unit B, piece 3	Background	2" x 3½"
Cardinal unit B, piece 4	Red #2	3¾" x 9½"
Cardinal unit B, piece 5	Black	1½" x 4"
Cardinal unit B, piece 6	Background	1¾" x 4¼"
Cardinal unit B, piece 7	Background	2½" x 2½"
Cardinal unit C, piece 1	Background	1½" x 3¾"
Cardinal unit C, piece 2	Brown	2" x 2"
Cardinal unit C, piece 3	Background	3½" x 5"
Bluebird unit A, piece 1	Blue	2¼" x 3"
Bluebird unit A, piece 2	Background	2¼" x 3"
Bluebird unit A, piece 3	Background	1" x 3½"
Bluebird unit B, piece 1	Background	2½" x 3½"
Bluebird unit B, piece 2	Brown	1½" x 1½"
Bluebird unit B, piece 3	Blue	2" x 2½"
Bluebird unit B, piece 4	Blue	1½" x 1½"
Bluebird unit B, piece 5	Background	2" x 2"
Bluebird unit C, piece 1	Orange/red	2½" x 4"
Bluebird unit C, piece 2	Background	2½" x 3½"
Bluebird unit C, piece 3	Blue	2½" x 4"
Bluebird unit C, piece 4	Blue	3" x 5½"
Bluebird unit C, piece 5	Orange/red	1½" x 2½"
Bluebird unit D	Background	7¼" x 7¼", cut in half diagonally
Bluebird unit E	Background	6¾" x 6¾", cut in half diagonally
Leaf units	Background and leaf fabrics	3¾" x 42" strips

Additional Cutting

Fabric	Used For	Number to Cut	Size to Cut		
			Twin	Queen	King
Green	Side borders	2 strips, cut on lengthwise grain	15½" x 63½"	15½" x 63½"	15½" x 63½"
Green	Top and bottom borders	2 strips, cut on lengthwise grain	15½" x 75½"	15½" x 84½"	15½" x 102½"

Piecing the Quilt Top

1. Refer to "Transferring the Patterns" on page 11 to prepare foundations for your blocks. The Cardinal block is made up of 3 units, A, B, and C. The Bluebird block is made up of 5 units, A, B, C, D, and E. Both bird block foundations are shown facing left, which means that the finished bird will be facing right. When you're making your foundation patterns, you'll also have to make some that face left, as indicated in the chart below. The foundation patterns are on pages 67–69.

   NOTE: *Remember that the pattern is a mirror image of the sewn block. To make a right-facing bird, use a left-facing pattern, and vice versa.*

Unit	Twin	Queen	King
Right-facing Cardinal blocks	8	12	16
Left-facing Cardinal blocks	9	9	12
Right-facing Bluebird blocks	12	12	16
Left-facing Bluebird blocks	6	9	12
Leaf units	70	84	112

2. Cut the fabrics as indicated in the cutting charts.

3. Refer to "Basic Paper Piecing" on page 12 to construct the Cardinal and Bluebird blocks. For the Cardinal block, stitch unit A to unit B, then attach unit C to complete the block. For the Bluebird block, join units A and B, then join them to unit C. Attach units D and E to complete the block.

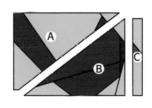 

Cardinal

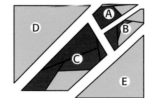 

Bluebird

4. To make the Leaf units, paper piece them with leaf fabrics in pieces 2 and 4, and the background fabric in pieces 1, 3, and 5. Stitch the Leaf units together into pairs, as shown.

Make 1 per bird.

5. Stitch a pair of Leaf units to the bottom of each bird block.

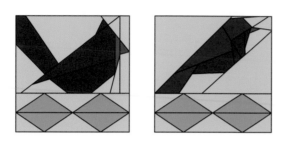

6. Following the quilt layout diagram, arrange the blocks into rows. The twin-size quilt has 7 rows of 5 blocks each, the queen-size quilt has 7 rows of 6 blocks each, and the king-size quilt has 7 rows of 8 blocks each. Stitch the rows together. Remove the paper from the seam allowances and press the seam allowances to one side as you go.

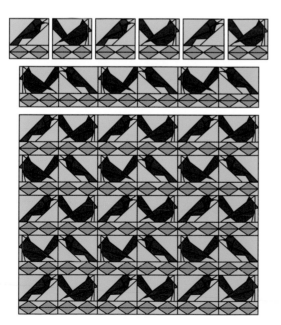

Quilt Layout
Queen-size

Borders

1. Stitch the side borders to the quilt top. Remove paper from the seam allowances and press the seam allowances toward the borders.

2. Stitch the top and bottom borders in place. Remove paper from the seam allowances and press the seam allowances toward the borders.

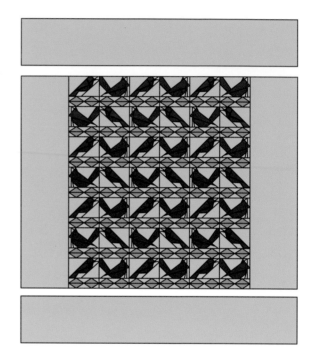

Finishing the Quilt

1. Remove the remaining paper from the blocks.

2. Add an eye to each bird, either by hand embroidering or sewing on a small button.

3. Referring to "Preparing for Quilting" on page 16, layer the quilt top, batting, and backing. Hand or machine quilt as desired. The quilt shown was quilted on a long-arm quilting machine with an allover Oak Leaves design (see "Resources" on page 77). Each row of the pattern was offset to add interest.

4. Trim the excess batting and backing from your quilt, and bind the edges following the instructions in "Making and Applying Binding" on page 17.

Diamond Windmill

Designed by Jodie Davis, 2001, Canton, Georgia, 84" x 93". Pieced by Joann Spiers, quilted by Sue Hunston.

Inspired by *a quilt I saw listed for sale on eBay, a popular Internet auction site, I designed my own version, using a variation of the Birds in the Air block. After making the quilt top using the traditional rotary-cutting method, I realized that if I'd paper pieced it I could have avoided having to match all those triangles. It occurred to me that other fervent paper-piecers would agree that removing paper is preferable to fretting over all those pesky points.*

✳✳✳

Quilt Sizes

	Twin	Queen	King
Finished quilt size	75" x 93"	84" x 93"	102" x 93"
Finished block size	9" x 9"	9" x 9"	9" x 9"
Number of pieced blocks	51	58	65
Number of alternate blocks	12	14	16

Materials *Yardages are based on 42"-wide fabric.*

	Twin	Queen	King
Assorted prints, totaling	6 yds.	7 yds.	8 yds.
Background	4½ yds.	5 yds.	6 yds.
Backing	5¼ yds.	7¾ yds.	9¼ yds.
Batting	83" x 101"	92" x 101"	110" x 101"

Cutting for Paper Piecing

To make paper piecing quicker and to minimize fabric waste, precut your fabrics for the paper-pieced units. Since some paper-piecers like to have more leeway with their fabric than others, make a sample block to determine if these measurements work for you before you cut all your fabric.

Fabric	Size to Rough Cut	Number to Cut
Assorted prints	5¼" x 42"	2 strips from each fabric
Background	5¼" x 42"	4 strips

Additional Cutting

Fabric	Used For	Size to Cut	Number to Cut		
			Twin	Queen	King
Background	Pieced blocks	9⅞" x 9⅞" ◺	51	58	65
Background	Alternate blocks	9½" x 9½"	12	14	16
Background	Borders	6½" x 42"	8	9	10
Assorted prints	Prairie points	4" x 4"	158	168	184

◺ = Cut squares diagonally once

Piecing the Quilt Top

1. Refer to "Transferring the Patterns" on page 11 to prepare foundations for your blocks. Each pieced block includes 2 pieced units, A and B, which are stitched together before they are joined to complete the block. You'll need to make 51 each of unit A and unit B for a twin-size quilt, 58 of each for a queen-size quilt, or 65 of each for a king-size quilt. The foundation patterns are on page 70.

2. Cut the fabrics as indicated in the cutting charts.

3. Refer to "Basic Paper Piecing" on page 12 to construct the A and B units.

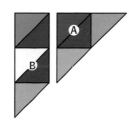

4. Stitch each unit A to a unit B.

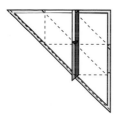

5. Stitch a 9⅞" background triangle to each pieced triangle. Press the seam allowances toward the background triangles.

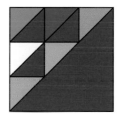

6. Following the quilt layout diagram, arrange the paper-pieced blocks and the 9½" background squares in rows. Stitch the rows together, then remove the paper from the seam allowances. Press the seam allowances toward the background squares.

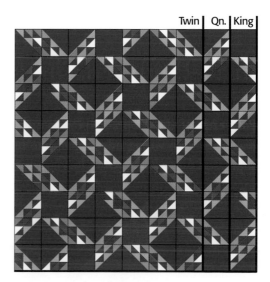

Quilt Layout

Borders

1. To make the borders, sew the border strips together end to end. Measure the length of your quilt top and cut the side borders to that measurement. Stitch the borders to the sides of the quilt top. Remove paper from the seam allowances and press the seam allowances toward the borders.

2. Measure the width of your quilt top and cut the top and bottom borders to that measurement. Stitch the borders in place. Remove paper from the seam allowances and press the seam allowances toward the borders.

3. Remove the remaining paper foundations from the backs of the blocks.

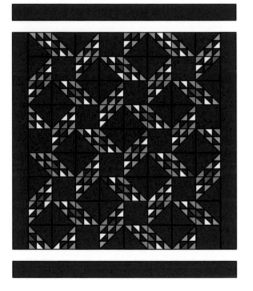

Prairie-Point Edging

1. Fold each of the 4" prairie-point squares in half diagonally with wrong sides together to form a triangle, and press. Fold each in half again and press.

2. Pin the prairie points to each edge of the quilt top, inserting each into the folds of the one next to it and making sure the open folds all face in the same direction. Adjust the spacing as necessary to fit the prairie points evenly on all sides of your quilt. Baste the prairie points in place.

Finishing the Quilt

1. Referring to "Preparing for Quilting" on page 16, layer the quilt top, batting, and backing. Hand or machine quilt as desired, being careful not to stitch too close to the edges of the quilt. You'll need to turn the quilt backing under to finish off the prairie-point edging, so keep stitches about ½" from the edges. The quilt shown was stitched in the ditch around the pieced triangles, then the background was filled with artistic freehand feathers and paisley meandering.

2. Trim the batting even with the basting stitches that hold the prairie points in place. Trim the backing fabric about ¼" larger.

3. Fold the edge of the backing fabric to the inside and slipstitch it in place.

Wedge Log Cabin

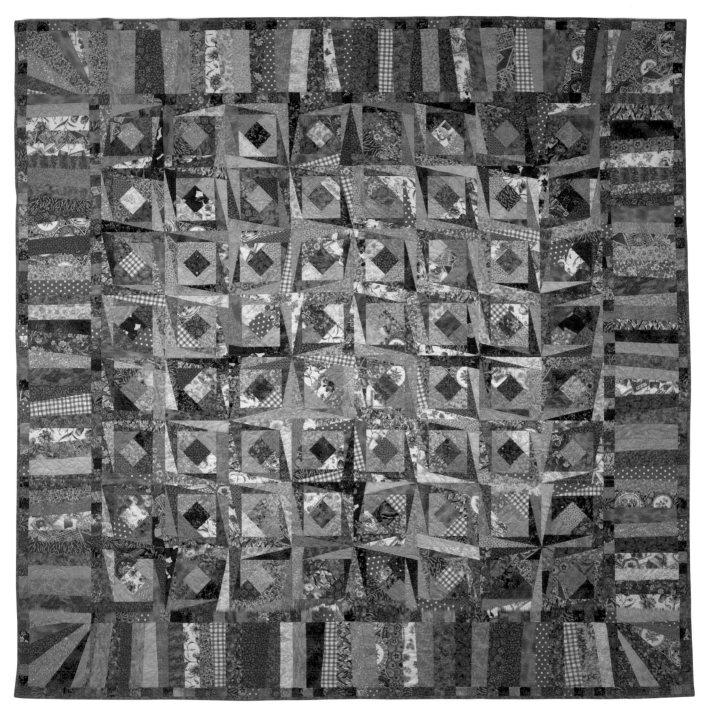

Designed by Jodie Davis, 2001, Canton, Georgia, 96" x 96". Pieced by Tammy Silvers, quilted by Glenda Irvine.

Although this *quilt looks complex, the simple cookbook approach to its construction makes it much easier than you might imagine. The recipe calls for so many of each type of block, you lay them out according to the plan, stitch them together, and voilà! This quilt is a great chance to use up (or buy!) fabrics in your favorite color. Don't worry over the fabrics you choose. I jumbled together bright, muted, and pale blues, and all sorts of patterns, but I think you'll agree that they work. Just gather your fabrics—aiming for a wide variety of colors, textures, and patterns—into one a pile of lights and one of darks, and get started.*

✳✳✳

Quilt Sizes

	Twin	Queen	King
Finished quilt size	84" x 84"	96" x 96"	106" x 106"
Finished block size	8" x 8"	9" x 9"	10" x 10"
Number of pieced blocks	64	64	64
Number of border blocks	40	40	40
Number of corner blocks	4	4	4

NOTE: *Only the 9" (queen size) block patterns are given. To make the 8" twin-size blocks, reduce the patterns to 89 percent on a photocopier. To make the 10" king-size blocks, enlarge the patterns to 111 percent.*

Materials *Yardages are based on 42"-wide fabric.*

	Twin	Queen	King
Assorted blue, totaling	11½ yds.	14 yds.	18 yds.
Assorted red, yellow, and orange, totaling	2 yds.	2½ yds.	2¾ yds.
Backing	7¾ yds.	8¾ yds.	9½ yds.
Batting	92" x 92"	104" x 104"	114" x 114"
Binding	¾ yd.	⅞ yd.	1 yd.

Cutting for Paper Piecing

To MAKE paper piecing quicker and to minimize fabric waste, precut your fabrics for the paper-pieced units. Since some paper-piecers like to have more leeway with their fabric than others, make a sample block to determine if these measurements work for you before you cut all your fabric.

Block	Piece	Size to Rough Cut
Wedge Log Cabin	1	4" x 4"
	2	3¾" x 42"
	3	5½" x 42"
	4	5½" x 42"
	5	5½" x 42"
	6	2" x 42"
	7	2" x 42"
	8	2" x 42"
	9	2" x 42"
	10	2" x 42"
	11	2" x 42"
	12	2" x 42"
	13	2" x 42"
Border		3" x 42"
Corner	1	2" x 6"
	2	2¼" x 8½"
	3	4" x 12"
	4	5" x 14"
	5	4" x 12"
	6	2¼" x 8½"
	7	2" x 6"

Additional Cutting

| Fabric | Used For | Size to Cut | Number to Cut | | |
			Twin	Queen	King
Assorted blues, reds, yellows, and oranges	Inner and outer borders	2½" x 2½"	300	336	372

Piecing the Quilt Top

1. Refer to "Transferring the Patterns" on page 11 to prepare the foundations for your blocks. You'll need to tape together the two halves of the Wedge Log Cabin block pattern before tracing or copying. Also join the two halves of the corner block pattern before tracing or copying. If you're making a twin- or king-size quilt, remember to reduce or enlarge your patterns before making the paper foundations. For any size of quilt, you'll need to make 64 Wedge Log Cabin foundations, 40 border block foundations, and 4 corner block foundations. The foundation patterns are on pages 71–74.
2. Cut the fabrics as indicated in the cutting charts.
3. Referring to "Basic Paper Piecing" on page 12, construct the blocks. To make the dark blue and red star design in the quilt, make your blocks according to the following color recipe:

   20 blocks with dark blue in sections 6, 7, 8, and 9
   16 blocks with dark blue in sections 2, 3, 4, and 5
   12 blocks with dark blue in sections 2, 3, 4, and 5, and red, yellow, or orange fabrics in section 9
   16 blocks with red, yellow, or orange fabrics in section 9

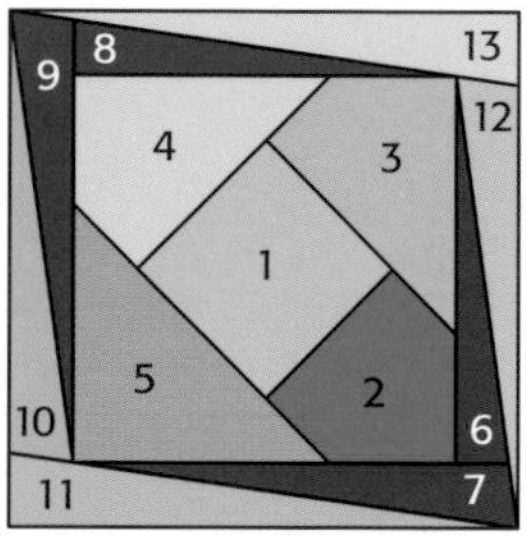

Make 20.

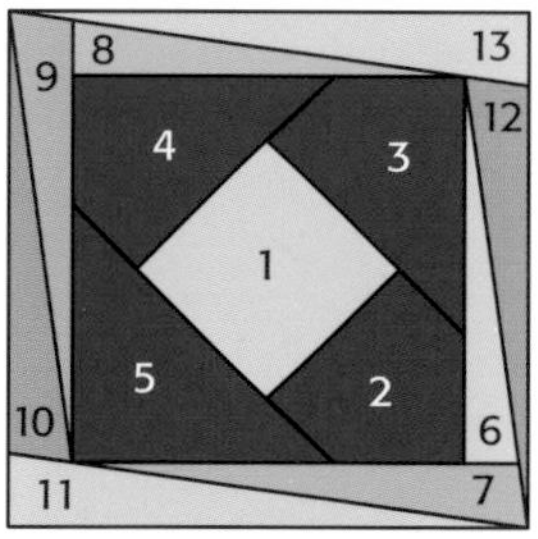

Make 16.

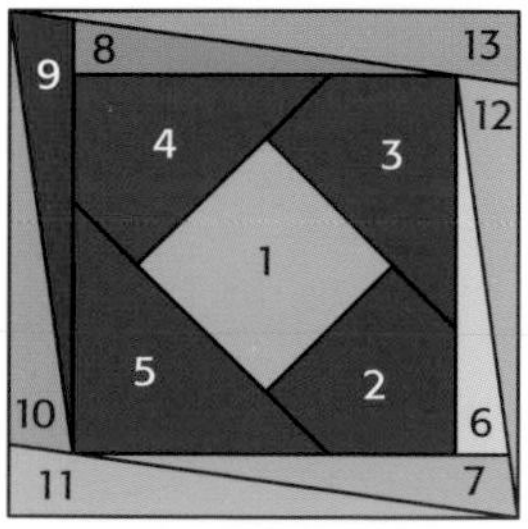

Make 12.

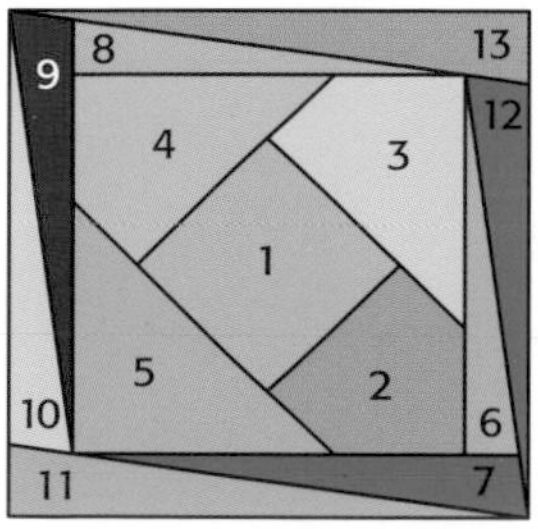

Make 16.

4. Make the corner and border blocks as shown.

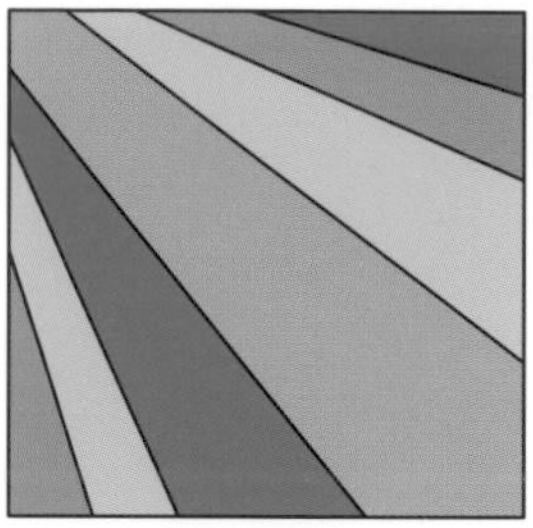

Corner block
Make 4.

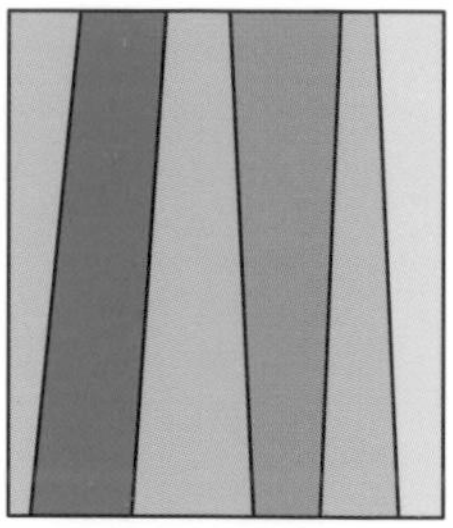

Border block
Make 40.

5. Referring to the quilt layout diagram for color placement, arrange the Wedge Log Cabin blocks into 8 rows of 8 blocks each. Stitch the blocks into rows, then remove the paper from the seam allowances. Press the seam allowances to one side. Stitch the rows together, and remove the paper from the seam allowances. Press the seam allowances to one side.

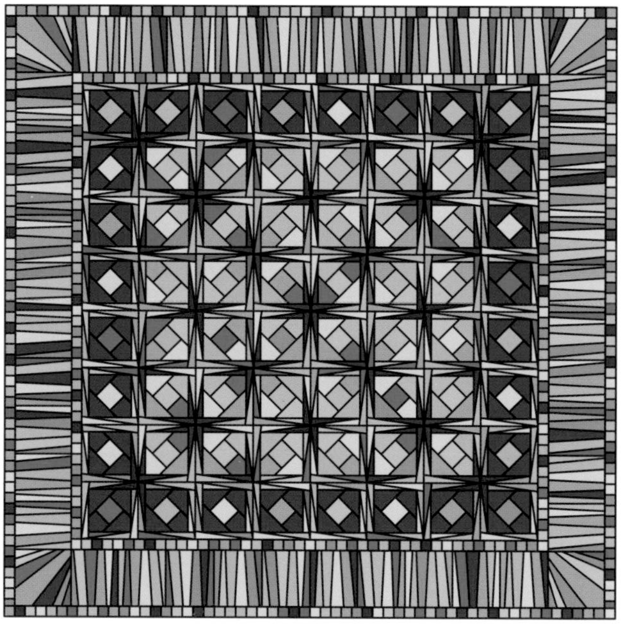

Quilt Layout

Borders

1. This quilt has inner, middle, and outer borders. To make the inner and outer borders, stitch the 2½" squares randomly into strips, following the chart below for the number of squares needed for each. Press the seam allowances of each strip in one direction.

	Twin	Queen	King
Side inner borders (make 2)	32	36	40
Top and bottom inner borders (make 2)	34	38	42
Side outer borders (make 2)	42	47	52
Top and bottom outer borders (make 2)	44	49	54

Make 4 inner borders.
Make 4 outer borders.

2. Stitch a side inner border to opposite sides of the quilt top. Press the seam allowances toward the center of the quilt.

3. Stitch the top and bottom inner borders to the quilt top. Press the seam allowances toward the center of the quilt.

4. To make the middle border, paper piece 40 border blocks and 4 corner blocks. Stitch 10 border blocks together to make a border. Remove the paper from the seam allowances and press the seam allowances to one side. Repeat to make 3 more borders.

Make 4 middle borders.

5. Stitch 2 of the middle borders to opposite sides of the quilt top. Remove the paper from the seam allowances and press the seam allowances away from the quilt center.

6. Stitch a corner block to each end of the remaining 2 middle borders. Remove the paper from the seam allowances and press the seam allowances away from the quilt center.

Attach corner blocks to top and bottom middle borders.

7. Referring to the quilt layout diagram on page 52, stitch the middle borders to the top and bottom of the quilt. Remove the paper from the seam allowances and press the seam allowances toward the outer borders.

8. To add the outer borders, stitch the side outer borders to the quilt, and press the seam allowances toward the quilt center. Stitch the top and bottom outer borders to the quilt, and press the seam allowances toward the quilt center.

Finishing the Quilt

1. Remove the remaining paper foundations.

2. Referring to "Preparing for Quilting" on page 16, layer the quilt top, batting, and backing. Hand or machine quilt as desired. The quilt shown was quilted on a long-arm quilting machine using the Chantilly Lace pattern (see "Resources" on page 77).

3. Trim the excess batting and backing from your quilt, and bind the edges following the instructions in "Making and Applying Binding" on page 17.

Potted Posies

Designed by Jodie Davis, 2001, Canton, Georgia, 86" x 90".
Pieced by Tammy Silvers and Jodie Davis, quilted by Glenda Irvine.

MARRYING A rosy floral with cozy hand-dyed fabrics creates a perfect harmony on this quilt. The dark background fabric really highlights the soft colors of the flowers and their terra-cotta pots. In a fun twist, prairie points are sewn inside the outermost border to create three-dimensional tops on the picket fence that surrounds this flowery garden.

* * *

Quilt Sizes

	Twin	Queen	King
Finished quilt size	66" x 90"	86" x 90"	106" x 108"
Finished block size	10" x 12"	10" x 12"	10" x 12"
Number of blocks	9	15	28

Materials *Yardages are based on 42"-wide fabric.*

	Twin	Queen	King
Terra-cotta hand-dyed for pots	½ yd.	1 yd.	1¼ yds.
Blue and pink hand-dyed for posies	9 squares, 5" x 5"	15 squares, 5" x 5"	28 squares, 5" x 5"
Green hand-dyed for leaves and border	2¾ yds.	2¾ yds.	3¼ yds.
Black tone-on-tone print for block background and border	3 yds.	4 yds.	5½ yds.
White tone-on-tone print for border and prairie points	3½ yds.	7½ yds.	9½ yds.
Black floral print for picket border	1½ yds.	4 yds.	5 yds.
Backing	7 yds.	8 yds.	9½ yds.
Batting	74" x 98"	94" x 98"	114" x 116"
Binding	¾ yd.	⅞ yd.	1 yd.

Cutting for Paper Piecing

To MAKE paper piecing quicker and to minimize fabric waste, precut your fabrics for the paper-pieced units. Since some paper-piecers like to have more leeway with their fabric than others, make a sample block to determine if these measurements work for you before you cut all your fabric.

Piece	Fabric	Size to Rough Cut
Unit A, piece 1	Blue and pink	4½" x 4½"
Unit A, pieces 2 and 3	Background	1¾" x 2¾"
Unit A, piece 4	Yellow	4½" x 4½"
Unit A, pieces 5 and 6	Background	4½" x 4½"
Units B and C	Green	3¼" x 42"
Units B and C	Background	3¼" x 42"
Unit D, piece 1	Terra-cotta	2½" x 7½"
Unit D, pieces 2 and 3	Background	2½" x 2½"
Unit E, piece 1	Terra-cotta	6¾" x 5¾"
Unit E, pieces 2 and 3	Background	3" x 5¾"

Additional Cutting

Fabric	Used For	Size to Cut	Number to Cut Twin	Number to Cut Queen	Number to Cut King
Black tone-on-tone print	Setting rectangles	6" x 42"	2 strips; cut strips into 8 rectangles, each 6" x 10"	4 strips; cut strips into 15 rectangles, each 6" x 10"	7 strips; cut strips into 28 rectangles, each 6" x 10"
Black tone-on-tone print	Side first borders	3½"-wide strips, cut on lengthwise grain	2 strips, each 54½" long	2 strips, each 54½" long	2 strips, each 72½" long
Black tone-on-tone print	Top and bottom first borders	3½"-wide strips, cut on length of grain	2 strips, each 36½" long	2 strips, each 56½" long	2 strips, each 76½" long
White tone-on-tone print	Pickets in third borders	3" x 42" strips; subcut into 3" x 11½" strips	19 strips, cut into 56 rectangles	43 strips, cut into 128 rectangles	55 strips, cut into 164 rectangles
White tone-on-tone print	Prairie points	3" x 42" strips; subcut into 3" squares	6 strips, cut into 56 squares	13 strips, cut into 128 squares	17 strips, cut into 164 squares

Additional Cutting (continued)

Fabric	Used For	Size to Cut	Twin	Queen	King
				Number to Cut	
Black floral print	Third borders	2½" x 42" strips; subcut into 2½" x 11½" strips	20 strips, cut into 60 rectangles	46 strips, cut into 136 rectangles	58 strips, cut into 172 rectangles
Green hand-dyed	Side second borders	2½"-wide strips, cut on length-wise grain	2 strips, each 60½" long	2 strips, each 60½" long	2 strips, each 72½" long
Green hand-dyed	Top and bottom second borders	2½"-wide strips, cut on length-wise grain	2 strips, each 42½" long	2 strips, each 56½" long	2 strips, each 80½" long
Green hand-dyed	Side fourth borders	2½"-wide strips, cut on length-wise grain	2 strips, each 90½" long	2 strips, each 90½" long	2 strips, each 108½" long
Green hand-dyed	Top and bottom fourth borders	2½"-wide strips, cut on length-wise grain	2 strips, each 64½" long	2 strips, each 72½" long	2 strips, each 102½" long

Piecing the Quilt Top

1. Refer to "Transferring the Patterns" on page 11 to prepare foundations for your blocks. Each block is made up of 5 paper-pieced units (A–E) which are stitched together before they are joined to complete the block. You'll need to make 9 of each unit for a twin-size quilt, 15 of each unit for a queen-size quilt, and 28 of each unit for a king-size quilt. The foundation patterns are on pages 75–76.

2. Cut the fabrics as indicated in the cutting charts.

3. Referring to "Basic Paper Piecing" on page 12, construct the Potted Posies blocks, making each of the A, B, C, D, and E units individually, then stitching them together into blocks. To set in the flower in unit A, piece 4, see "The V Technique for Inset Pieces" on page 14.

Potted Posies block

4. Following the quilt layout diagram, arrange the blocks and the setting rectangles. Sew the blocks and rectangles into vertical rows. Remove the paper from the seam allowances, and press the seam allowances in one direction. Sew the rows together, remove the paper from the seam allowances, and press the seam allowances in one direction.

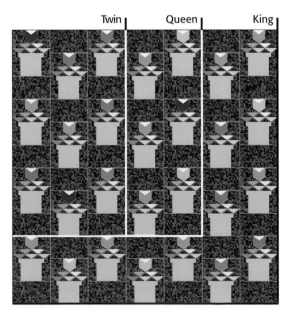

Quilt Layout

Borders

1. This quilt has 4 borders. To make the first border, stitch a black tone-on-tone print border to each side of the quilt top. Press the seam allowances toward the borders. Repeat with the top and bottom first borders.

2. To add the second border, stitch a green hand-dyed side border to each side of the quilt top. Press the seams toward the first border. Repeat with the top and bottom second borders.

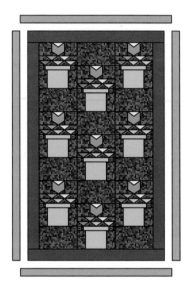

3. To make the third border, lay out pieces for the picket-fence border according to the chart below, alternating black floral strips with white tone-on-tone strips, and beginning and ending on each side with a black floral strip. Sew the strips together into 4 borders. Press the seam allowances toward the black floral strips.

	Twin	Queen	King
Side borders:			
Black floral strips	15	15	19
White tone-on-tone strips	14	14	18
Top and bottom borders:			
Black floral strips	14	19	24
White tone-on-tone strips	14	18	23

Third border
Make 4.

4. Pin the 2 side third borders to the sides of the quilt top, centering them along the quilt edges. Stitch. Press the seam allowances toward the second borders.

5. Pin and stitch the top and bottom third borders to the quilt top in the same manner. Press the seam allowances toward the second borders.

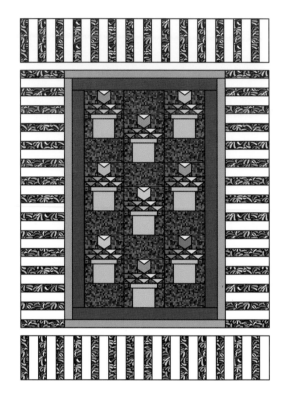

NOTE: *If you are going to quilt this quilt with a long-arm machine, quilt it now, before adding the prairie-point picket tops and the fourth border. Be sure to allow at least 8" of backing and batting beyond the edges of the quilt top for the addition of the fourth border. Also, don't quilt right to the edge; leave ¾" to 1" free.*

6. To add the fourth border, begin by making prairie points. Fold a 4" square in half, wrong sides together, to form a triangle, and press. Fold in half again to make a prairie point. Press again. Pin the prairie point to the raw edge of a white picket strip in the third border. (Note: The corners of the prairie point will extend beyond the sides of the picket. Once the seam is stitched, the corners of the prairie point should meet the sides of the picket.) Repeat

for the remaining pickets. Baste the prairie points in place.

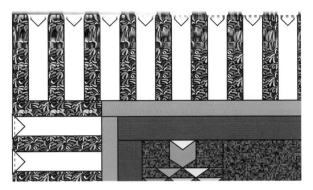

Baste prairie points in place.

7. Stitch the green top and bottom fourth borders to the quilt top. Press the seam allowances toward the third borders and the picket tips toward the fourth borders.

8. Stitch the side fourth borders to the quilt top and press in the same manner.

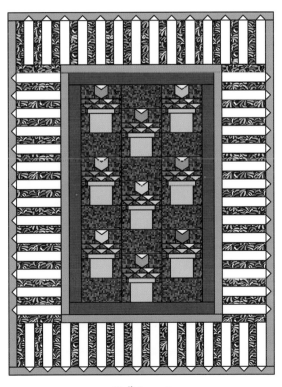

Quilt Layout

Finishing the Quilt

1. Remove the remaining paper foundations.

2. Referring to "Preparing for Quilting" on page 16, layer the quilt top, batting, and backing. Hand or machine quilt as desired. The quilt shown was quilted on a long-arm quilting machine using the Rose Vine and Wildflower patterns in the borders (see "Resources" on page 77). A large freehand stipple design was used around the pots to let the piecing stand out. Individual roses from the border design were quilted on the terra-cotta pots.

3. Trim the excess batting and backing from your quilt, and bind the edges following the instructions in "Making and Applying Binding" on page 17.

Patterns

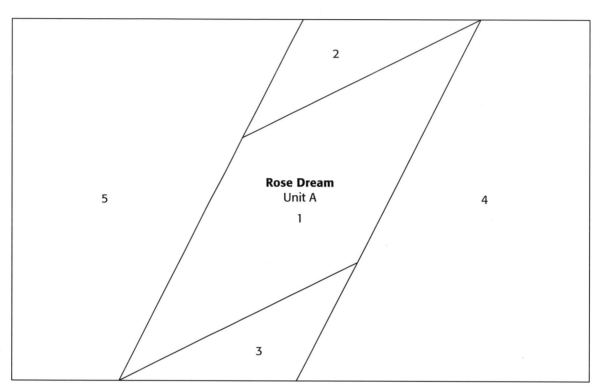

Rose Dream
Unit A

5

2

1

4

3

Add ¼" seam allowance when
trimming around completed units.

Rose Dream
Unit B

1

2

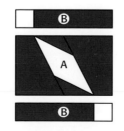

Rose Dream block

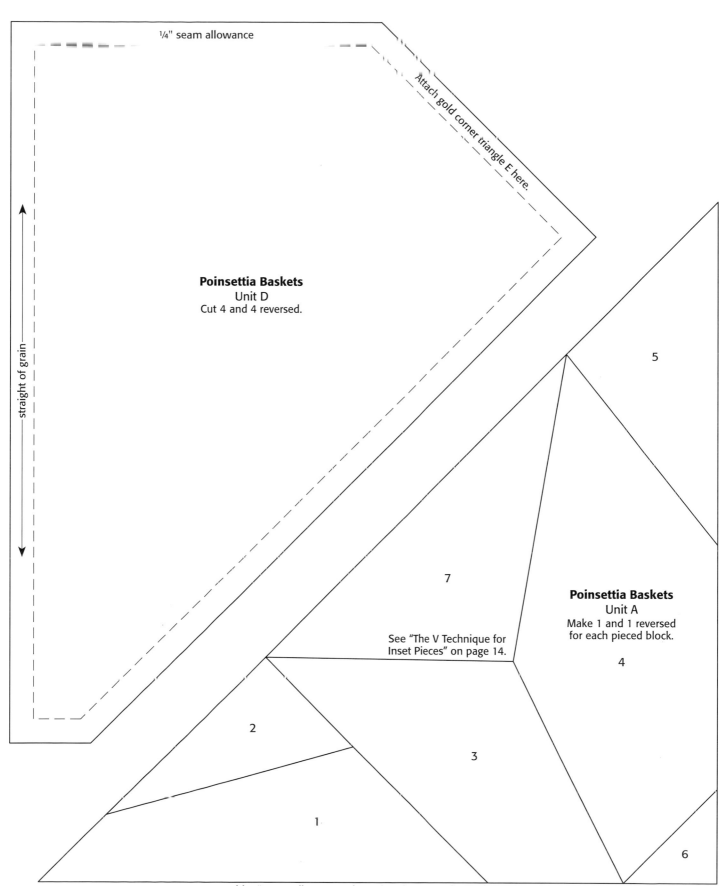

¼" seam allowance

Attach gold corner triangle E here.

straight of grain

Poinsettia Baskets
Unit D
Cut 4 and 4 reversed.

5

7

See "The V Technique for
Inset Pieces" on page 14.

Poinsettia Baskets
Unit A
Make 1 and 1 reversed
for each pieced block.

4

2

3

1

6

Add ¼" seam allowance when trimming around completed unit.

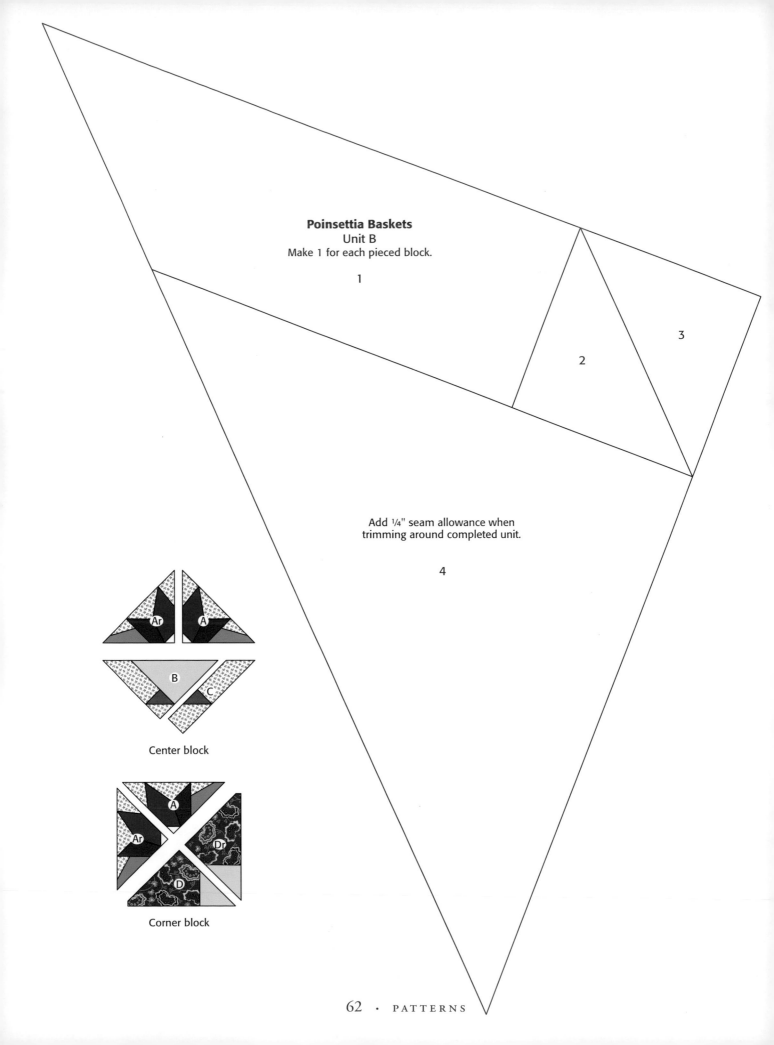

Poinsettia Baskets
Unit B
Make 1 for each pieced block.

1

2

3

Add ¼" seam allowance when
trimming around completed unit.

4

Center block

Corner block

Poinsettia Baskets
Unit C
Make 1 for each pieced block.

1

Add ¼" seam allowance when
trimming around completed unit.

2

3

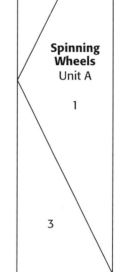

**Spinning
Wheels**
Unit A

2

1

3

Add ¼" seam allowance when
trimming around completed units.

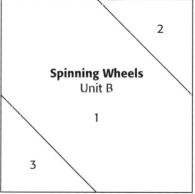

Spinning Wheels
Unit B

2

1

3

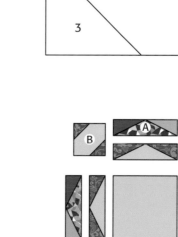

Spinning Wheels block

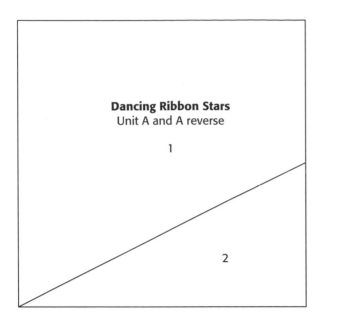

Dancing Ribbon Stars
Unit A and A reverse

1

2

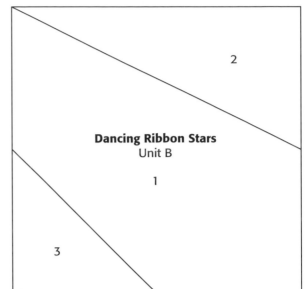

2

Dancing Ribbon Stars
Unit B

1

3

Add ¼" seam allowance when
trimming around completed units.

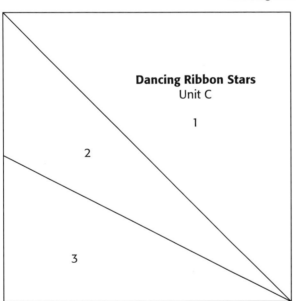

Dancing Ribbon Stars
Unit C

1

2

3

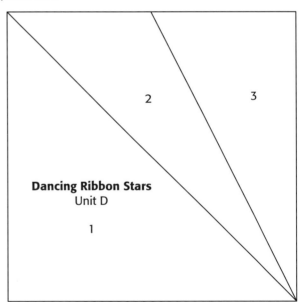

2

3

Dancing Ribbon Stars
Unit D

1

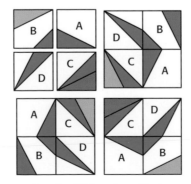

Dancing Ribbon Stars block

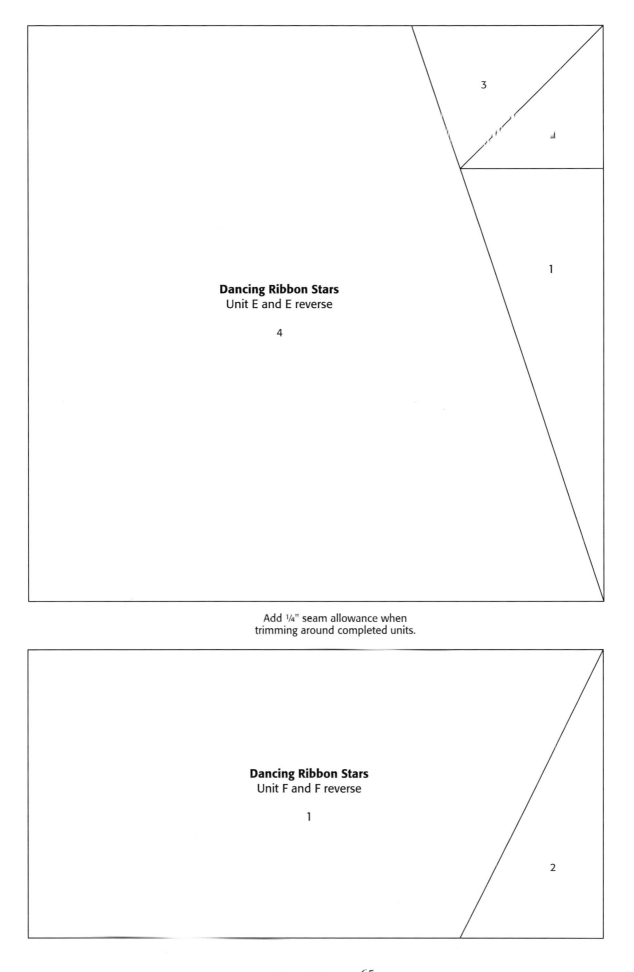

Dancing Ribbon Stars
Unit E and E reverse

4

3

⌐

1

Add ¼" seam allowance when
trimming around completed units.

Dancing Ribbon Stars
Unit F and F reverse

1

2

Dancing Ribbon Stars
Unit G

1

2

3

Add ¼" seam allowance when trimming around completed unit.

Songbird Serenade

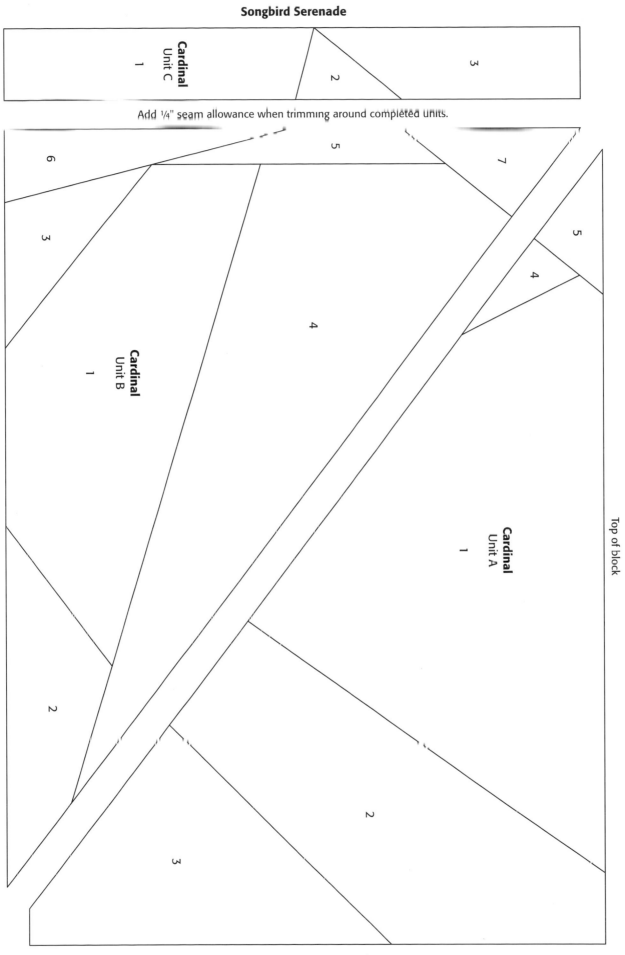

Add ¼" seam allowance when trimming around completed units.

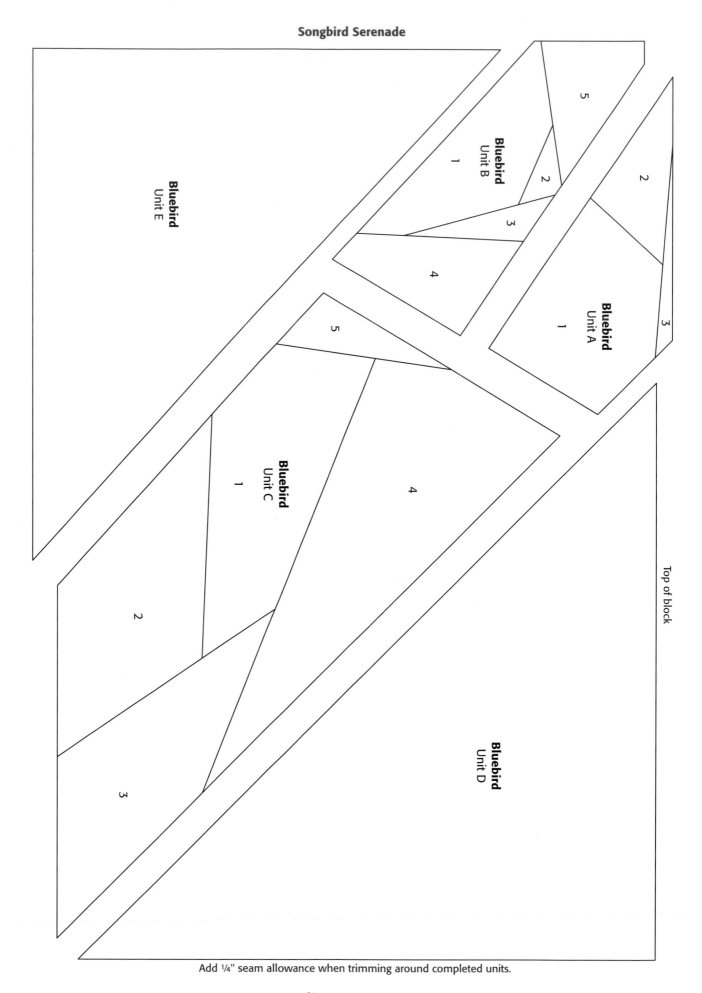

Add ¼" seam allowance when trimming around completed units.

Songbird Serenade

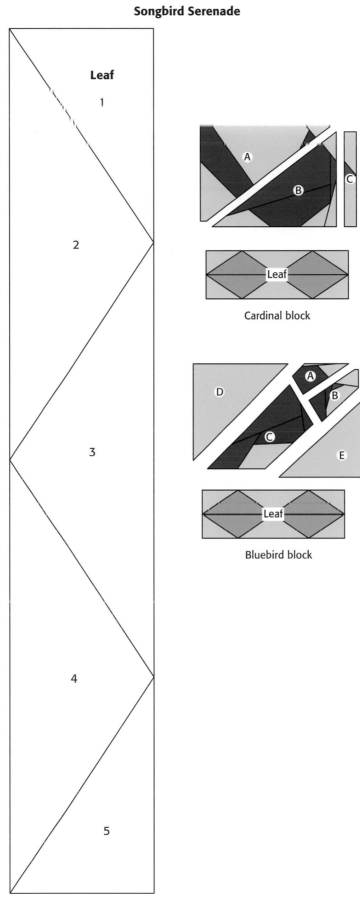

Leaf

1

2

3

4

5

A

B

C

Leaf

Cardinal block

A

B

C

D

E

Leaf

Bluebird block

Add ¼" seam allowance when
trimming around completed unit.

Add ¼" seam allowance when trimming around completed units.

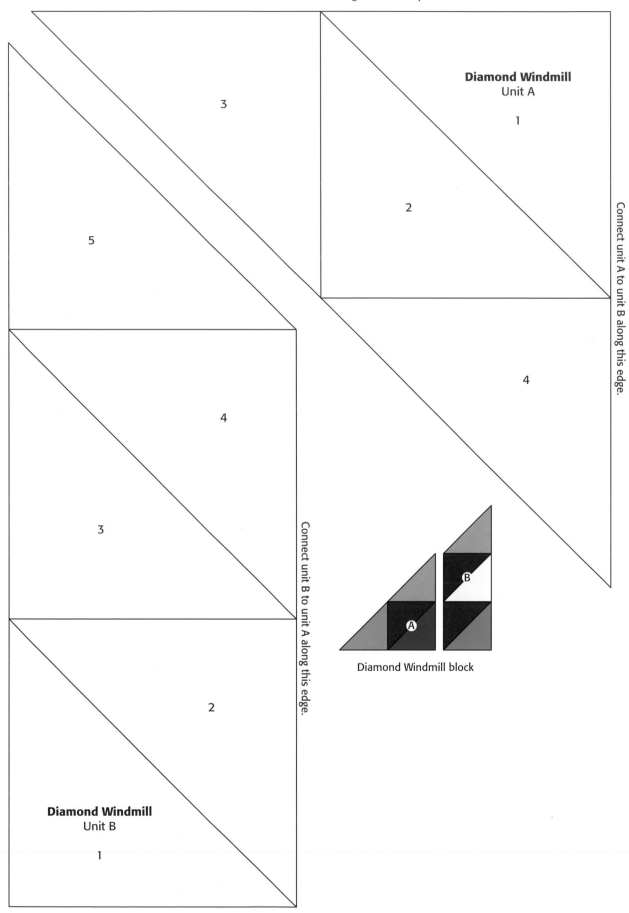

3

Diamond Windmill
Unit A

1

2

5

Connect unit A to unit B along this edge.

4

4

3

Connect unit B to unit A along this edge.

2

Diamond Windmill block

Diamond Windmill
Unit B

1

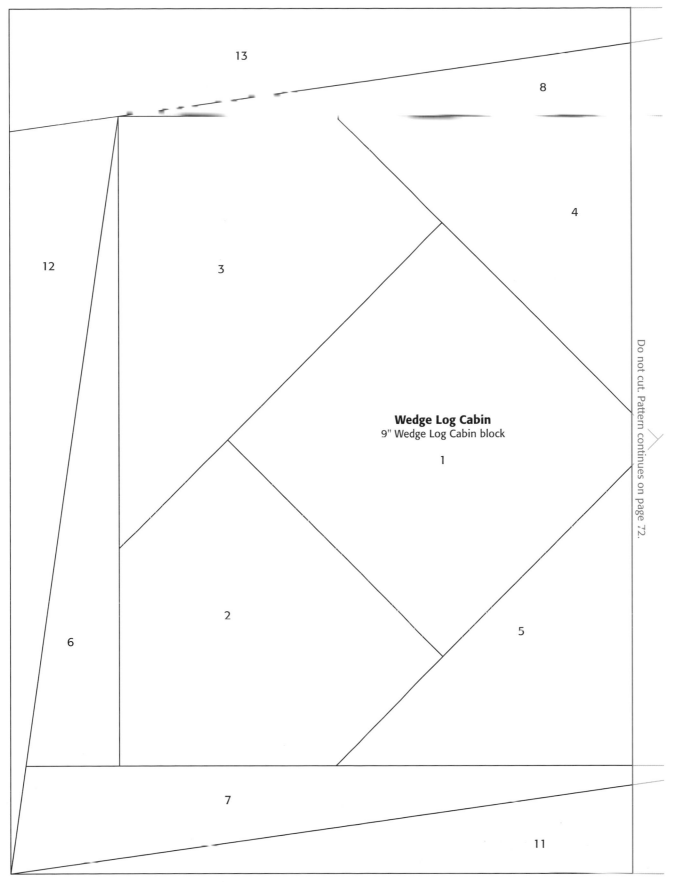

Wedge Log Cabin
9" Wedge Log Cabin block

Do not cut. Pattern continues on page 72.

Add ¼" seam allowance when trimming around completed units.

Pattern is for 9" x 9" finished block (queen-size quilt). For 8" x 8" finished block (twin size), reduce pattern to 89%. For 10" x 10" finished block (king size), enlarge pattern to 111%.

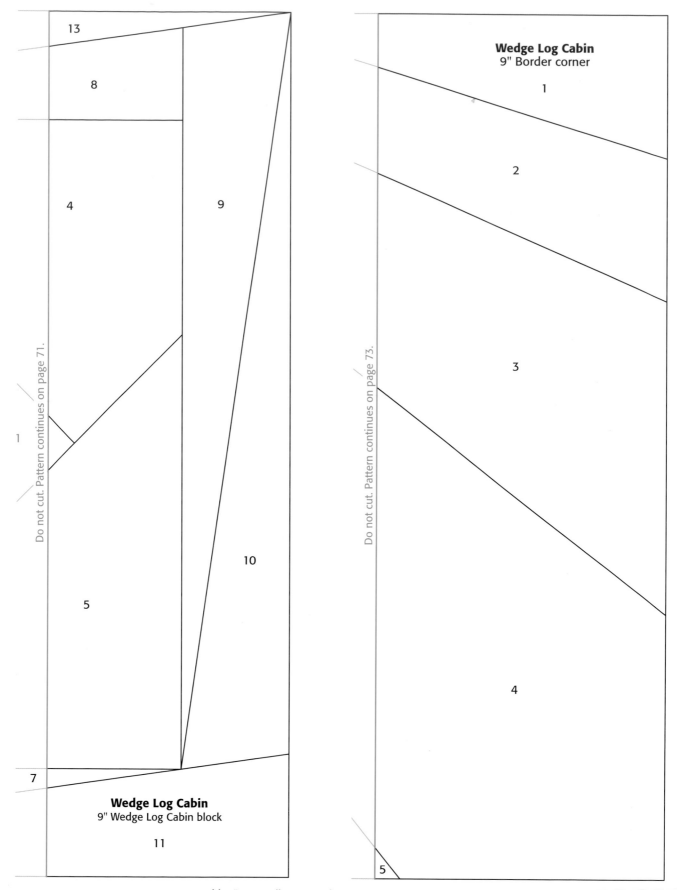

13

8

4

9

Do not cut. Pattern continues on page 71.

1

5

10

7

Wedge Log Cabin
9" Wedge Log Cabin block

11

Wedge Log Cabin
9" Border corner

1

2

3

4

Do not cut. Pattern continues on page 73.

5

Add ¼" seam allowance when trimming around completed units.

Patterns are for 9" x 9" finished block (queen-size quilt). For 8" x 8" finished block (twin size),
reduce pattern to 89%. For 10" x 10" finished block (king size), enlarge pattern to 111%.

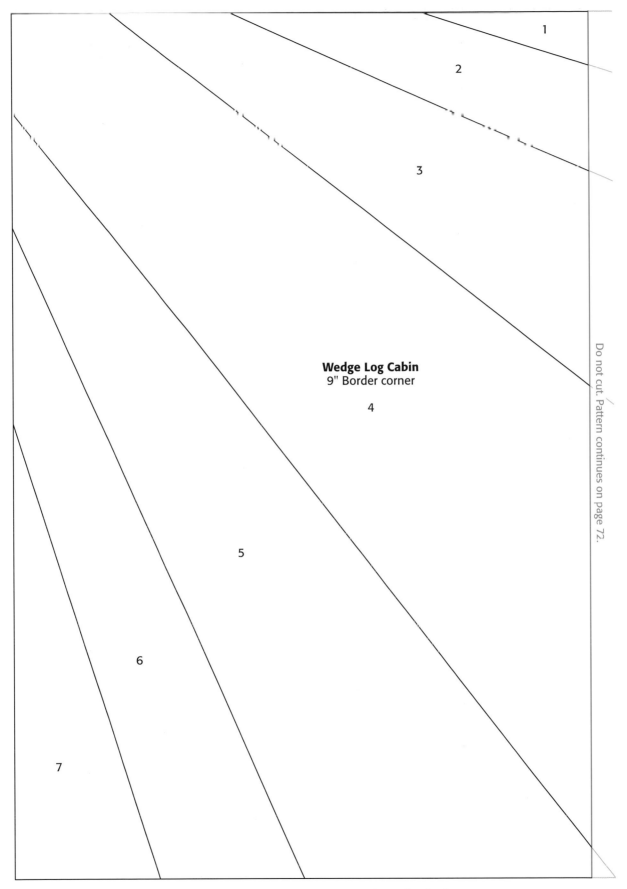

1

2

3

Wedge Log Cabin
9" Border corner

4

5

6

7

Do not cut. Pattern continues on page 72.

Add ¼" seam allowance when trimming around completed units.

Pattern is for 9" x 9" finished block (queen-size quilt). For 8" x 8" finished block (twin size),
reduce pattern to 89%. For 10" x 10" finished block (king size), enlarge pattern to 111%.

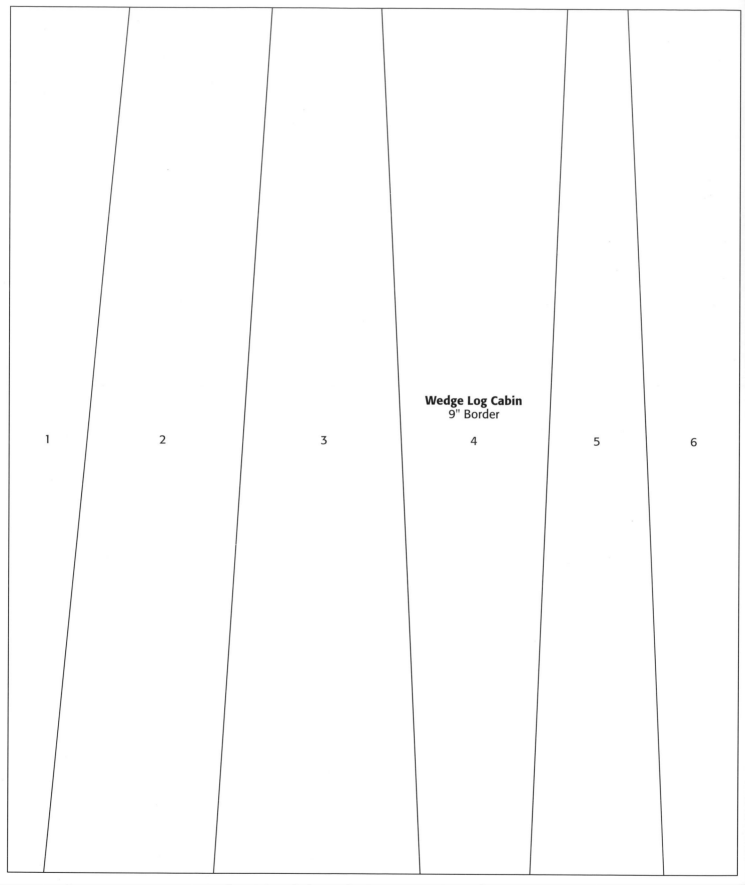

Wedge Log Cabin
9" Border

1   2   3   4   5   6

Add ¼" seam allowance when trimming around completed units.

Pattern is for 9" x 9" finished block (queen-size quilt). For 8" x 8" finished block (twin size),
reduce pattern to 89%. For 10" x 10" finished block (king size), enlarge pattern to 111%.

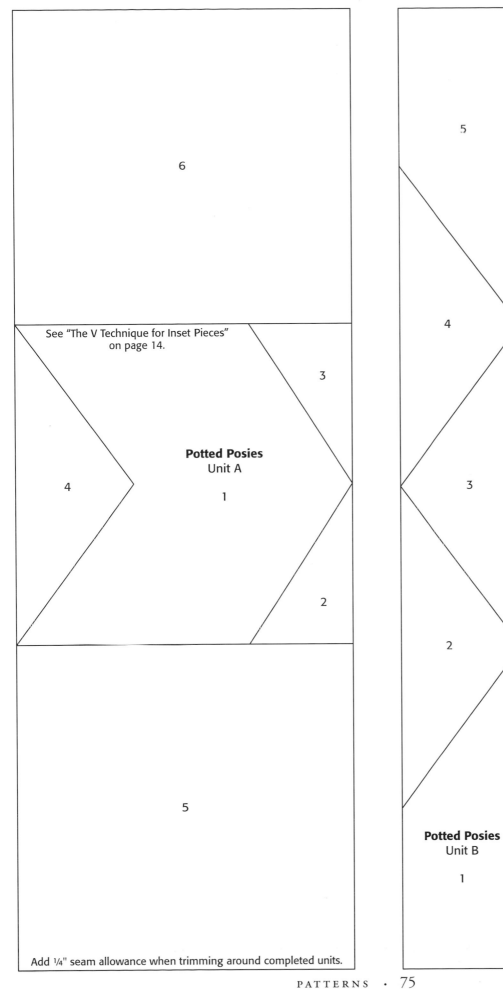

6

See "The V Technique for Inset Pieces"
on page 14.

3

Potted Posies
Unit A

4

1

2

5

Add ¼" seam allowance when trimming around completed units.

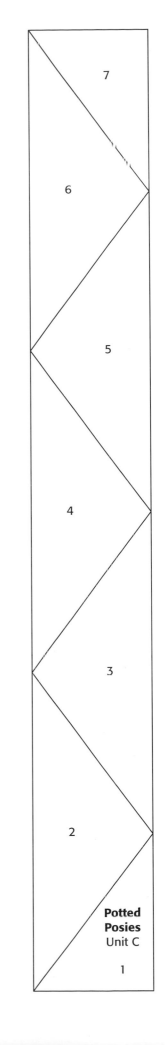

7

5

6

4

3

5

4

2

4

3

Potted Posies
Unit B

1

2

Potted Posies
Unit C

1

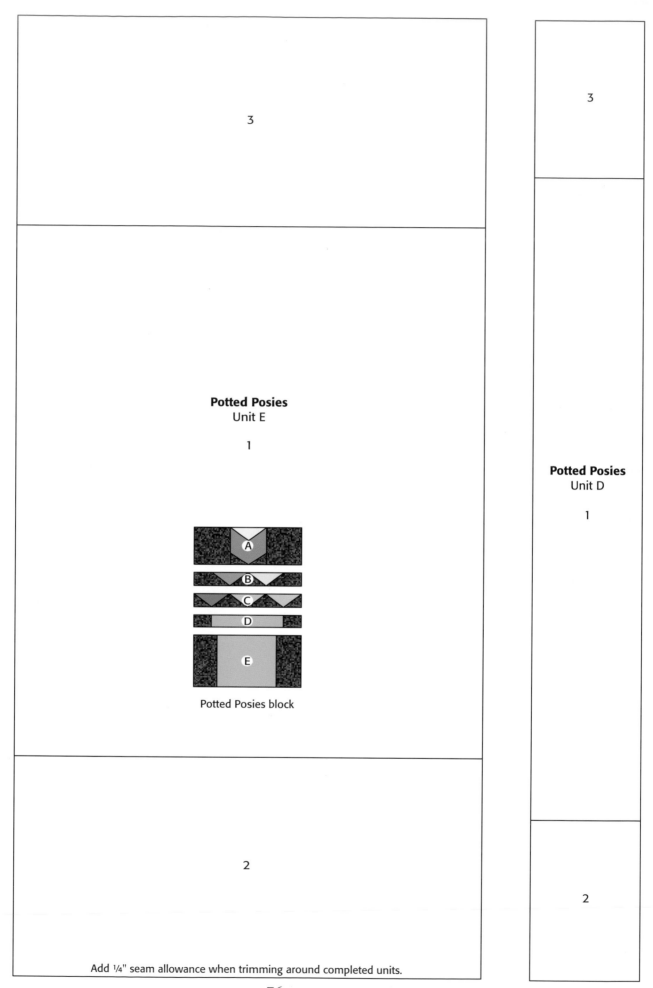

Potted Posies
Unit E

3

1

Potted Posies block

Potted Posies
Unit D

1

2

3

2

Add ¼" seam allowance when trimming around completed units.

Resources

Mail-Order Shopping

NOTHING BEATS visiting a quilt shop to see all the latest luscious fabrics and sewn samples and to enjoy the camaraderie of fellow quilt lovers. Believe me, I help my local shops thrive! But there are never enough fabrics and quilting goodies for my appetite, so I often use mail-order and online quilting sources. Here are the resources I use and recommend without hesitation.

Big Horn Quilts
608 Greybull Avenue
P.O. Box 566
Greybull, WY 82426
877-586-9150
www.bighornquilts.com

At this online fabric store, fabric certainly does take center stage. Big Horn Quilts offers lots of it, all at prices that are hard to resist.

Connecting Threads
P.O. Box 8940
Vancouver, WA 98668-8940
800-574-6454
www.connectingthreads.com

Connecting Threads has recently launched a great Web site full of books, patterns, fabrics, and most every quilting tool imaginable, all at discounted prices.

eQuilter
4581 Maple Court
Boulder, CO 80301
303-516-1615
www.eQuilter.com

Specializing in Asian-Pacific and contemporary fabrics, eQuilter owner Luana Rubin worked all over Asia as a textile and fashion designer and now brings her love of Asian textiles home to American quilters.

Hancock's of Paducah
3841 Hinkleville Road
Paducah, KY 42001
800-845-8723
www.Hancocks-Paducah.com

A delicious selection of the latest fabrics from the best manufacturers and designers, plus threads, quilting gadgets, batting, and more, all at great prices. Check out both the online and paper catalogs, since one may have fabrics the other doesn't.

Keepsake Quilting
Route 25B
P.O. Box 1618
Center Harbor, NH 03226
800-525-8086
www.keepsakequilting.com

Keepsake Quilting's hefty little catalog is chock-full of all the latest and tried-and-true quilt notions, gadgets, patterns, books, and fabric, along with handy fabric medleys. No wonder it's titled "The Quilter's Wishbook"!

PineTree Quiltworks, Ltd.
585 Broadway
South Portland, ME 04106
207-799-9535
www.quiltworks.com

A complete quilt shop, including a wonderful selection of fabrics and every ruler and other notion imaginable, all at discounted prices. PineTree Quiltworks also offers a traditional mail-order catalog.

Quilt-a-way Fabrics
540 Back Westminster Road
Westminster, VT 05150
802-722-4743
www.quiltaway.com

A full-service quilt shop, Quilt-a-way's mail-order site offers a great selection of fabrics, including many batiks, at the lowest possible prices.

Quilts and Other Comforts
1 Quilters Lane
P.O. Box 4100
Golden, CO 80401-0100
800-881-6624
www.quiltsonline.com/quilts

"The catalog for quilt lovers" focuses on fabrics and patterns, with a good selection of the most popular books and all those wonderful quilt tools as well. You'll also find some nice quilty gift items.

Hand-Dyed Fabrics

To obtain the hand-dyed fabrics I used in "Potted Posies," contact Tammy Silvers at tamarini@juno.com.

Quilting Patterns

Gammill Quilting Systems
www.gammill.net

Click on the "Supplies" button and you'll find stencil patterns for the Folk Lily quilting design used for "Poinsettia Baskets," Oak Leaves used for "Spinning Wheels," Chantilly Lace used for "Dancing Ribbon Stars" and "Wedge Log Cabin," scallop and double feather used for "Rose Dream," Rose Vine and Wildflower used for "Potted Posies," and the Circle-Ease used for the pieced center of "Spinning Wheels."

Golden Threads
2 South 373 Seneca Drive
Wheaton, IL 60187
800-477-7718
www.goldenthreads.com

You'll discover more block, border, whole-cloth, and theme quilting designs for long-arm machines at this Web site, as well as stencils, patterns, and notions for hand quilting.

ONLINE SHOPPING TIP

❊

I order online frequently, and feel confident doing so by using the secure server. (It's very easy, just follow the online instructions.) But if you're not convinced this is safe, do your shopping online, print out the order, and call the company with your order and credit-card information. Online orders are acknowledged with e-mail messages telling you your order was received, what was ordered, and the total amount. Most companies also send you an e-mail when your merchandise is sent. Pretty neat! If you think online ordering is impersonal, have no fear; quilters just like us who love quilts run these businesses. I have corresponded with each of them and heard only excellent reviews from other online quilters.

When fabric shopping online, I right-click my mouse on the swatch on my screen, click "Copy," and go to my draw program and paste it. After I audition the fabrics I print my thumbnail swatches. This way, I not only have a visual record of what I order but can staple the printouts to my quilt design so I know exactly how I intended to use them in the quilt.

Other Online Resources

Following are a few starting points for exploring quilting and foundation piecing in the wonderful world of cyberspace.

About.com
www.quilting.about.com

The mission of About.com is to be the place to go to learn about any topic. Each site is devoted to a specific area of interest and is hosted by a real, live, accessible human being. And Susan Druding's quilting site fulfills the mission perfectly. It's a resource for all facets of quilting, offering how-tos, FAQs, sources, links to other sites, and more.

FoundationPiecers
www.smartgroups.com/groups/foundationpiecers

Dedicated specifically to foundation piecing, the FoundationPiecers site has a lot of great information, patterns, and activities, as well as links to many other foundation-piecing sites and goodies.

Judy Smith's Quilting, Needlearts and Antiques Page
www.quiltart.com/judy

Judy is an online quilter from way back and has a highly acclaimed site of great quilting links. Starting your search with Judy's site, you'll quickly accrue a long list of bookmarked favorites!

Zippy Designs Publishing
Home of *The Foundation Piecer*
R.R. 1, Box 187M
Newport, VA 24128
540-544-7128
www.zippydesigns.com

Yes! There is a magazine devoted exclusively to foundation piecing. The creation of husband-and-wife team Stephen Seifert and Elizabeth Schwartz, *The Foundation Piecer* is a lovely, full-color bimonthly, featuring inspired patterns.

And don't miss the Zippy Designs Web site. You'll find a schoolhouse of foundation-piecing instructions, block patterns, information about the magazine, products, and much more.

The following are other great starting places.

Planet Patchwork
www.planetpatchwork.com

Quilt Channel
www.quiltchannel.com

QuiltNet
www.quilt.net

World Wide Quilting Page
ttsw.com/MainQuiltingPage.html

About the Author

SINCE HER first book debuted in 1988, Jodie has been enjoying creating her quilt, teddy-bear, and doll designs with crafters all over the world through more than two dozen books. Never afraid to try the not-so-traditional, Jodie has embraced the ease of paper piecing and shares her love of the technique with such titles as *Paper-Pieced Curves, Paper Piece a Merry Christmas,* and *Paper Piece a Flower Garden.*

Living in north Georgia with her husband, Bill, four cats, one Dalmatian (is enough!), and an Indian Ringneck parakeet, Jodie also enjoys collecting rubber duckies and cuckoo clocks, and growing orchids and African violets. She and her husband spend weekends caring for a yard chock-full of every plant they can possibly fit in their space.

To see what Jodie is up to currently, visit her at her Web site, www.iejodie.com.